THE MOUNTAIN PATH

ALSO BY PAUL PRITCHARD

The Totem Pole, Deep Play and The Longest Climb.

THE MOUNTAIN PATH

A CLIMBER'S JOURNEY THROUGH LIFE AND DEATH

PAUL PRITCHARD

Vertebrate Publishing, Sheffield
www.adventurebooks.com

THE MOUNTAIN PATH

PAUL PRITCHARD

First published in 2021 by Vertebrate Publishing. This paperback edition first published in 2022.

 Vertebrate Publishing
Omega Court, 352 Cemetery Road, Sheffield S11 8FT, United Kingdom.
www.adventurebooks.com

A CIP catalogue record for this book is available from the British Library.

ISBN: 978-1-83981-093-0 (Paperback)
ISBN: 978-1-83981-094-7 (Ebook)

10 9 8 7 6 5 4 3 2 1

Cover design by Nathan Ryder, Ryder Design.
www.ryderdesign.studio

Production by Cameron Bonser, Vertebrate Publishing.
www.adventurebooks.com

Printed and bound by Lightning Source.

For Eli Gareth

CONTENTS

Between the sun and the moon, the restless desire to live and the restless desire to die, the mountain holds the balance.

— Etel Adnan, *Journey to Mount Tamalpais*

FOREWORD
BY HAZEL FINDLAY

I heard of Paul long before I met him, and read his book *The Totem Pole* long before I climbed the sea stack after which the book is named. Paul's accident didn't put me off wanting to climb the matchstick pinnacle found seemingly swaying in the swell of the Tasman Sea. It probably sounds weird to someone who doesn't climb that I would be interested in climbing a piece of rock that almost took someone's life, but the Totem Pole is an improbable exemplar of rock architecture and speaks directly to the desires that make a climber who they are.

When I first saw the Totem Pole, I wondered how it hadn't already fallen into the ocean. And when I started climbing the narrow splinter of rock, I questioned how I could climb it without pushing it over. When I gained the halfway ledge, my mind imagined the seven painful and lonely hours Paul had spent there, leaking blood and cerebral fluid after being hit in the head by a laptop-sized rock. He left half his blood and who knows how many brain cells on that ledge, but in his own words he 'gained eighty years of wisdom'.

My first impression of Paul was one of fragility. He is unable to use half of his body very well due to his hemiplegia, and his speech is slow and laborious due to his damaged frontal lobe. All this could lead you to think Paul vulnerable. That's until you look him in the eye, and you see an inner strength unique to someone who's skirted death three times. Like the Totem Pole, it's easy to mistake Paul's outer image with one of fragility, but there is a resilience to Paul that seems impervious to the turbulent waves of life. That said, he has none of the dullness or arrogance of many ageing mountaineers; he giggles like a child, especially at himself.

Since the age of six, I've bent myself towards climbing, like a tree edging towards the light. I'm also a fond reader of books. Despite being a lover of climbing and a lover of books, I rarely enjoy climbing novels or the biographies of great climbers. They always seem dull, egotistical and inadequate at depicting the complexity of our relationship with climbing. I consider them to advertise all the negative aspects of masculinity, a shallow repetition of the hero's journey without the heart and vulnerability of the climber's life as I experience it. Perhaps for some, the challenge of climbing is about achievement, about making our egos bigger. I wanted to read about the real worth of challenge and a hero's battle to dismantle the ego.

At some point *The Totem Pole* landed under my nose and this book did captivate my attention. Perhaps because it's a story of losing climbing, it does a better job of getting close to why we do it. It's also a story about how the worst thing that could happen can become the best thing, which in reality is a story of acceptance, growth and courage. And I could relate to a story like that.

In my twenties, a shoulder injury stopped me from climbing for a while and I had to work out how to be happy without climbing. Some chain of events that I won't go into landed me in a Vipassana meditation centre and it was there that I learnt the real nature of happiness as a condition of the mind, dependent on inner strength and not external conditions. After Paul's accident, he ended up taking the same course and in *The Mountain Path* Paul does well to explain how mind-blowing ten days of sitting on your arse and doing nothing can be.

For Paul, acceptance should have been harder. Prior to his accident, he was one of the best climbers in the world and travelled to many exciting mountains around the globe. He had gone from climbing some of the hardest routes to relearning how to walk and talk. His accident had effectively made him a baby again. I guess if you can accept that, you can accept anything.

Meditation is a method of training the mind in acceptance; unfortunately, it's not that fun. Climbers are lucky because the mountains are also great teachers. With the right mindset, experiences in the mountains that require presence and control of our primal pain and fear bring with them great wisdom. In these environments, we go through a mental boot camp and come out the other side stronger. In *The Mountain Path* you'll read about these lessons through the eyes and emotions of someone who's not only had to learn acceptance the hard way, but also continues to practise this applied wisdom in his ongoing relationship with the mountains and adventures as a disabled person. You'd think that living with a disability, hemiplegia, seizures and fits would be challenging enough, but Paul's boundless curiosity to better understand himself has propelled him around the world on various challenges including a 1,100-kilometre trike journey across Tibet to Everest Base Camp.

The mountains are a kind of schoolroom for those who want answers more quickly than the rest and who are curious to see the depths of the self, however painful. The problem is that it doesn't matter how perfect the schoolroom or how brilliant the teacher, the student needs to be ready and willing to learn. For those of you who've spent your lives in the mountains, maybe ignoring the lessons available to mountaineers and climbers, then I imagine this book could be a diving board for inner inquiry. For those who are already on the path, this book is probably something you've long been waiting for. Paul lays out the spiritual lessons we can learn on the mountain path with humour and humility. Paul's experiences in the mountains and his brushes with death make him the perfect author for this book.

Hazel Findlay, *hazel-findlay.com*

INTRODUCTION

Never regret thy fall,
O Icarus of the fearless flight
For the greatest tragedy of them all
Is never to feel the burning light.

— Oscar Wilde (attributed)

'You've not washed your feet, have you?' I joyfully castigated Steve after face-planting on his bare left foot. There had been no other way for my hemiplegic body to wriggle onto the rock needle's postage-stamp summit. My one functioning arm was almost useless after the 126 one-arm pull-ups it had taken me to get to the top of the Totem Pole.

My own legs were still stuck out over the void but here was the rest of me, on top of the world, kissing my dear leader's feet. He put out his hand and helped me to an unstable standing position, my legs fatigued and spastic. After a joyful hug I thought it best to sit down again and conduct operations from a cross-legged posture. Steve checked his knots and zipped himself across the rope we had rigged up earlier to connect us to the headland.[1] I was left alone, like Simeon Stylites, a lone figure on an ever-so-gently swaying pillar of dolerite, meditating on what I had just achieved.

It took a while to sink in. Eighteen years of learning and effort to get

---

1   Climbers call this a Tyrolean traverse, rigged to pull themselves across a void.

here, but I had just climbed the slenderest sea-stack in the world. At sixty-five metres, the Totem Pole is three times taller than Cleopatra's Needle in Central Park or Victoria Embankment (they are identical). And, at four metres square, only twice as wide. It stands in the Southern Ocean on a remote stretch of coastline in southern Tasmania. A local car bumper sticker reads: 'An island off an island, at the arse end of the world.'

Almost two decades earlier I had endured the most painful, lonely and confusing experience of my life on this stack of rock. My partner Celia Bull and I were attempting to free-climb this tower when a laptop-sized piece of dolerite scythed through the air from twenty-five metres above me and struck my skull like a blow from an axe. I was left hanging upside down on the end of the rope, just above the sea, blood pissing out of my head and turning the sea red.

Celia, standing on the Totem Pole's only ledge, now faced her own ocean of trauma as she hauled me back up the vertical wall, the nine-millimetre nylon rope gouging her hands. Bear in mind this was before the days of mobile phones. There was no dialling a rescue here. It took a full three hours before she could tie me safely to the ledge. Then she told me she was going to have to leave and get some help.

Fighting to steady her body, Celia began climbing the rope that we had left in place to the summit of the tower. She then clipped herself on to our zip-line connecting the pole to the mainland. Dragging herself across, she paused for breath, sixty metres above the swell that was now mauling the base of the column.

In a moment of morbid fascination, I walked my fingers up through my sticky hair to the top of my head. I discovered a huge hole in my skull. Shocked, I pulled my hand away. My fingers were painted red with blood and sticky with cerebrospinal fluid. The whole right side of my body had no feeling; I couldn't move either my arm or leg. When I tried to call Celia's name, no sound came from my mouth, just a faint croak. I was alone and broken on a distant stack of rock in the Southern Ocean.

Even though I had no idea why my limbs were paralysed, there was one thing I did know: I could trust Celia with my life, even though, as I was acutely aware, that life seemed likely to end soon. There was little I could do about that. And in my confused state, I had little energy for reviewing my life. I seemed comfortably detached about my imminent demise. All I could do was calmly accept my fate and make my last moments as un-distressing as possible. At the same time, I had to keep my options open. Here was a thought: what if I lived?

Drifting in and out of consciousness, I remember thinking, 'What the hell am I doing here?'

I know I didn't *just* mean 'What am I doing on this ledge?'

I knew that much.

I was now oblivious to Celia, as she climbed the final steep path to the crest of the headland above. It would take her two hours to run back to Fortescue Bay and trigger the rescue. Later, she told me that she had looked back at me down on that ledge and thought it was the last time she was ever going to see me alive.

* * *

Okay, I will pause at this rather dramatic moment – with me expiring on the ledge and Celia running to mobilise a rescue – to let you, the reader, know that I have already written two books about this piece of rock and the accident I suffered there. These books were first-hand, seat-of-your-pants accounts of the accident and my year in hospital.

My aim with this book is for you and me to go on an arduous pilgrimage of self-discovery, to compare notes of our highs and lows. This journey will not be comfortable or safe, I guarantee. But the chances are that it will change the way you see things, if only a little bit. The events recounted in this book certainly changed my life in a profound manner.

I have learnt much from the wild places I have wandered through and the mountains I have climbed, or failed to climb, including two previous near-death falls. I doubt I would have survived that day on the Totem Pole, spilling half my blood into the ocean and on to that ledge, without that knowledge gained in the mountains. I can still hear the vacant groaning as the air escaped my lung, as if Celia was dragging someone else inch by painful inch up that wall.

There, on that ledge, all I wanted to do was go to sleep. And I was certain that if I did drift off, it would be for the last time. I made a vague pact with myself to at least attempt to live. I found myself dumbly forcing my body up on to my one functioning elbow, looking down into a sticky red pool and moaning. I then dropped my head straight into my own sticky, cold blood with a dull thud. I don't want to gross you out but to communicate that without this persistent determination I would not have realised half the things I have done since. I very much doubt I would have attempted to climb Kilimanjaro or cycle to Everest. It is not stubborn or aggressive, this determination that The Mountain taught me. No. It is more a patient resolve.

I had to stay awake and alert, and yet remain calm and balanced also. Looking back from a distance of over twenty years I can now see that the meditative trance I entered into, neither asleep nor awake, was a vital coping mechanism. When we are in life-or-death situations, being paralysed with fear does *not* come naturally. In 1844, when a lion mauled David Livingstone, he thought it the most serene moment of his life. Like Livingstone, I was not overly worried about paralysis or death. I remained in a becalmed state of mind on that sofa-sized ledge for seven long hours before I sensed someone by me. No, not Jesus (or any other god for that matter), but he was my saviour, a paramedic named Neale Smith. Neale thought he was in for a simple corpse recovery judging by the amount of blood he saw on the ledge on his way down to me. When he saw that I was still alive, he knew there was no time to lose.

In the mountains, I believed I was embracing the true meaning of freedom, not the illusory freedom of following my passion; but until the Totem Pole, following my passion is all I did. I ditched the joinery apprenticeship I began at the age of sixteen and went climbing – every day – until my skull was split open fifteen years later. Afterwards, I discovered there is a greater freedom than this. There is a greater freedom.

Some might think that my near-death experience could have been easily avoided. If only I had ignored my passion and stuck with the apprenticeship in the suburbs of Manchester. Even so, a life spent working with wood, however attractive to some, was not for me. And as I'll explain, and I hope I can convince you, living with paralysis all these years has actually improved my life. So much so that I can say without doubt that this catastrophic brain injury is *the* single best thing that ever happened to me. It has given me a new perspective on life. It has led me to a markedly different philosophy.

Brain trauma is starkly different from any other form of injury. This isn't just what you could become. This is what you *really* are: the constant public fretting, the addictive behaviour, the verbalising of thoughts about sex. The emotional lability that forces you to see the hysterically funny side of death one moment, when the next you have tears streaming down your face because you have seen early morning storm-light caught on a tree. Always being in a variety of states of existential crisis. And very obvious states too. This is who we really are once we drop the façade, once we cease to act out the part we have created for ourselves.

The version of our lives that's like being trapped in *Waiting for Godot*.

Added to this, the partial long-term memory loss I suffered and an almost complete lack of working memory meant I was forced to live in the moment. In my mind, the loss of one's memory can be a curse or a meditation, for meditation is all about being in the present moment. I was forever grasping at the straws of times past that have, well, passed. It was exhausting. But I learnt that if I could accept that *this* was the reality of *this* moment, I could turn memory loss around so that it became an advantage. Don't get me wrong, though. I still have embarrassing moments in cafes when I am ordering breakfast. I can picture an egg but can't for the life of me recall the name for it and simply say, 'Egg, please.'

So instead I say, 'One of those oval things that come from chickens.'

Those who have brain injuries hold up a mirror to society. This can make brain-injured people terrifying to the 'normal' person in the street because at some level they fear this is who they might be. There are awkward reactions from some people, sideways glances and weird comments, day in, day out. Some of them I'm sure are meant as compliments. 'You're so brave,' they say, when I'm simply walking down a country path. Or else the comments are dressed as empathy. 'Never mind, I'm so forgetful too.'

Sometimes it's darker. People with disabilities often arouse suspicion. On more than one occasion I have been challenged while taking pictures of my son at soccer or looking for my daughter in the school grounds. I won't go into the psychology of why most Bond villains have a disability. But it's lucky that I have a black sense of humour and can see the funny side of these moments.

Occasionally it gets really dark. I have suffered physical attacks more than once. In the most recent, I was taking my children to a matinee performance of *The Wind in the Willows* at a local theatre. My lurching gait must have attracted the attention of a man who, unprovoked, crossed the street and punched me around the ear, knocking me to the ground. My already fragile head hit the pavement with a thud. After bending over me and urging me to 'fuck off and die', the man hurried off around the corner. A passer-by helped me to my feet. The apples I had slung around my shoulder in a bag were smashed. The only saving grace was that my kids were already in the theatre so didn't see their dad getting bullied.

So, I have dealt with some shit that nobody should ever have to face. And through this process, but in a more measured way than having a boulder crush my skull, I have been led down a different path of thought. Why do people behave as they do? Should I forgive my attacker? Perhaps they are just mistaken, as no one is born mean-spirited. What are the ethics of any given situation?

I think this constant questioning of reality forces you to take a philosophical journey. It certainly did me. And it's a journey encompassing many perspectives, not least a clearer interpretation of fear. Fear does not warrant the importance many of us attach to it. That doesn't mean we should not be concerned for our own welfare; just that whether we are paralysed with fear or not, the result will most likely be the same. What is courageous is the ability to trust that the universe will provide. Eleven years after my brain injury, I made my first lead climb since the accident. Clearly, it might have been safer to stay on the ground and not risk my neck. Yet I understood there was an opportunity for growth up there on The Mountain. So, we climb anyway. And as the years passed, I discovered this courage to be the essential and often difficult skill of living in the present and letting the future go without anticipation.

It wasn't until I embarked on a pedal-powered journey across the Tibetan Plateau that I realised what being in the present moment actually entailed. In Tibet I became aware that I was not nearly as important as I thought I was. And it was while turning my pedals monotonously round on the road to Everest that I understood the transformative effect pilgrimage can have on our lives.

The monotony of cycling across Tibet provided me welcome space for introspection. I was able to recall thousands of beautiful and terrifying experiences in the mountains. Looking down upon a blue glacier, all scaly and winding, from a rock tower in Pakistan, as if I were gazing for the first time at the sort of satellite imagery we see so commonly now on Google Earth ... Hanging alone on a mile-high wall in Patagonia, with just a thin cord disappearing into swirling white clouds above and below me ... Clinging to a Welsh slate face, held only by my fingertips; thirty metres above jagged rocks, knowing that one false move would be the end of me ... Brocken spectres on the Eiger in the Swiss Alps ... Footsteps in the bog all aglow with phosphorescent algae on the Isle of Lewis ... Or the red orb of the midnight sun, seen from a wall on Baffin Island.

Through the course of many discussions with our Tibetan guide and the monks I met along the plateau, I came to see that many of the people in Tibet had a similar worldview to the one I had learnt, by a sort of osmosis, in the mountains. I realised that through facing my deepest fear on The Mountain I was learning to live in the moment, a core teaching embodied in Buddhist philosophy.

* * *

After spending what had felt like eternity on that ledge, I became aware that I was being clipped to my rescuer's harness. Then I was being abseiled into a boat being tossed about by the waves. As the swell rose, Neale cut the rope and we both fell into this boat, which raced me to a helicopter waiting on the beach. It was all quite exciting, really.

When I arrived in hospital, the surgeon had to work through the night to save my life. Thus began, in 1998, the longest expedition I would ever go on. I am still on it. And it is the resilience and faith in myself fostered through years of rock climbing and mountaineering that stood me in good stead for the challenge of my second life.

* * *

During a whole year spent in a Merseyside hospital after my rescue I seemed to skip the five stages of grief. I never went through a denial stage. I never thought from my wheelchair, 'What's the point of it all?' I was never angry with the Totem Pole or myself. I never asked, 'Why me?' I never bargained with any god or whispered my 'if onlys' into the night.

However, I did descend into a deep depression at the thought of never being able to climb again. Recently, author David Roberts reminded me of the time he came to interview me in Wales for *National Geographic Adventure*. I had just written *The Totem Pole* and had won mountaineering literature's biggest prizes, the Boardman Tasker and the Grand Prize at the Banff Mountain Book Festival, so I was hot news. He drove me out to my heart cliff, Gogarth, on the island of Anglesey. I hobbled to the cliff edge and there, sitting among the sea pinks, looking down at the surging swell of the Irish Sea, puffins and guillemots wheeling across the crag's face, I broke down and sobbed for what I had lost.

But why climb in the first place? After all, there are a thousand reasons not to climb a mountain. Rockfall, hypothermia, avalanche, altitude sickness, the risk of falling off, severe weather or just the hard work of it all. When I looked at it carefully, I saw there is but one singular reason to climb a rock or mountain. It may be the most beautiful mountain you ever saw. It may be in a remote corner of the world you always wanted to visit. It may be a futuristic-looking line aching to be climbed, or you may want to ascend it simply for the exercise and the view from the top. It doesn't matter what the reasons are. The reason we climb is for the challenge.

That may sound trite. 'Of course it's for the challenge!' I hear you say.

But this challenge has questioning at its heart, and this questioning is fundamental if we wish to live our lives to the utmost. This challenging ourselves and questioning, if we do it often enough, pushes us to do our best, to be our best, to strive to be more comfortable with inevitable fears, to be more trusting and more able to be dedicated. It enables us to put painful events such as illness, grief and loss into perspective, and, dare I say it, live a more harmonious life.

So, despite my depression, in a few short months I had climbed out of that deep well of despair and accepted my situation. How was this possible? I suspected it was something to do with having spent my life in the mountains. If I was right, what was it that The Mountain had taught me? What was it about wild places that instilled in me such resolve? And, what was it about The Mountain that infused me with such acceptance of change and such an embrace of the most profound change of all: death?

What concerns me is not how to climb a mountain, but how The Mountain can help us sort out what the hell life is about. This is not a how-to manual. You will not find within these pages advice on mental conditioning or physical techniques for climbing mountains. Nor is The Mountain a simple Nietzschean metaphor for the triumph of the will, where the valley equals mediocrity and the summit fulfilment.

What fascinates me is just how The Mountain and moving upon it in an attentive way can be a doorway to transcend the material world. Back in 1987, I was making the scariest crag climb of my life at Gogarth. I was in a very precarious position where a slip could have spelt the end for both myself *and* my partner (who had great trust in me). Suddenly, I was telescoped out of my body. I became a separate consciousness watching myself climb, flowing through moves with assured certainty, and then – bam! – I crashed violently back into myself at the end of all difficulties.

Many climbers, in extremis, have had out-of-body experiences like this. The 'peak-experience', as Maslow would call it.[2] There are many such doorways to transcendence: painting or poetry, chess or dancing. However, the unique blend of nature's power and the uncertainty of success, or even of one's personal safety, combined with the mindfulness needed to be a climber, makes The Mountain unique.

When I hear the wind on The Mountain, a longing to climb tears at my heart, as if it is calling to me. When you listen to a mountain, quietly, with care, this longing reveals itself. When we spend time in the mountains, we do not escape from our woes. We come home and learn how to accept them.

This book, then, is a personal reflection on my relationship with The Mountain and the qualities this partnership has fostered within me, to meet a new life with new challenges at each moment. Those lessons learnt in the mountains got me through a harrowing injury and painfully slow recovery. I use them still, repeatedly, each day of my second, radically different life. And it is these lessons that enabled

---

2   Psychologist Abraham Maslow coined the term 'peak-experience' in his 1964 book *Religions, Values, and Peak-Experiences*.

a return to the Totem Pole eighteen years later to finally confront the tower in the sea that did me so much harm. And yet, paradoxically, made my life so much better.

1
FREEDOM

The journey goes down, not up. It's as if the mountain pointed toward the centre of the earth instead of reaching into the sky. Instead of transcending the suffering of all creatures, we move toward the turbulence and doubt. We jump into it. We slide into it. We tiptoe into it. ... At our own pace, without speed or aggression, we move down and down and down. With us move millions of others, our companions in awakening from fear. At the bottom we discover water ... Right down there in the thick of things we discover the love that will not die.

— Pema Chödrön, *When Things Fall Apart*

When I was a child, my mother used to take me hillwalking, adventuring all over the United Kingdom. The Pennines surrounded our home on the moors, so I would explore them on a daily basis. Sometimes we went on longer trips, to the English Lake District or to Eryri (Snowdonia) in Wales. However, it was on the Isle of Arran in Scotland that I got my first real taste of how an inanimate object such as a mountain can be both a companion and a mentor.

My mother would have been about forty years old then. Younger than I am now as I sit at my desk recalling this, some might say, foolish adventure. I would have been around the age of eleven and in my first year at secondary school. This particular walking holiday was to be my first experience of the dedication that comes with fear. And, through this fear, brought about by my mother and me risking our lives, I felt free, truly free, for the first time in my life.

Back home in Bolton, a grimy, fast-becoming-ex-mill town on the Lancashire moors, I would pore over my mother's collection of hiking guidebooks, mostly Alfred Wainwright's famous pictorial fell-walking guides. My mother had a sizeable collection of this beloved son of Lancashire's books on her shelf, with their finely detailed, exquisite black-and-white ink drawings … hundreds of them … thousands of them.

I had seen a meticulous sketch of the dangerous 'Witch's Step' in Wainwright's then-new book, *Scottish Mountain Drawings Volume Six*. I was very much intrigued by the formation, Ceum na Caillich in Gaelic, a deep slash on the ridge of Caisteal Abhail at the head of Glen Sannox on the Isle of Arran. 'The Step' requires a certain level of adeptness at rock climbing to traverse it successfully. I became obsessed and begged my mother to take me there. Fortunately, Arran held fond memories for her, of a time when she and my father were happy together. Mum and Dad had gone to the island on their honeymoon and hiked up Goat Fell, its highest peak. So she agreed. Mum's blue Datsun was packed to the gunnels with gear for a week's hostelling.

Only now, writing this, do I realise just how brave she was.

The day before our adventure, I'd almost perished in a swan attack. In those days, I kept an egg collection, carefully arranged in an Airfix Lancaster Bomber box. I had them embedded in sawdust, in ranks, smallest to largest, from wren to chaffinch to mistle thrush and Canada goose. But I had yet to procure the smallest egg in Britain, the goldcrest, and, as every schoolboy knew, the largest – a mute swan. Now I spied a magnificent mute swan on her nest at the head of an inlet on Loch Ranza.

My father had told me that Captain Webb lathered himself in Vaseline for his swim across the Channel. Since I didn't have any, I applied a liberal coating of Vicks VapoRub over my body instead. And then I swam – or did my best approximation of swimming, since there's little call for it on the Lancashire moors – out into the frigid waters of the loch. The single mother was off her nest as I approached. And although the VapoRub was doing a splendid job of wicking heat away from my body, I could hardly contain my excitement as I eyed a clutch of six of the fabled white eggs in the huge nest. Breathing hard and barely treading water, I then heard a fearful honking from behind and received a sharp blow to the back of my head. I turned to find the immense white mother had blotted out the sky. Half drowning, I thrashed my way back to shore, and that was the last time I ever attempted to purloin a wild bird's egg.

My mother and I arose early next morning and ate our soft-boiled hens' eggs in the deserted youth hostel kitchen. The mist was lying low to the sunlit fields and wrapping itself around the ruin of Loch-ranza Castle out on its spit. We parked the car at the entrance to Glen Sannox and started to walk. I behaved like an excited dog, belting ahead and then trotting back to tell 'me mum' about a grouse up ahead, or a colourful flower.

We made the summit in no time and once there wandered around the surreal granite tors in quickly congealing cloud. When we had started, the morning was hot and perfectly still with just a few wispy cirrus. Now the wind was driving grey water vapour through the summit castellations with some force. We huddled behind one of the granite blocks and ate a chewy muesli bar while the wind increased in strength. The fabled Witch's Step was only a short distance away. I could see the ridge abruptly cease and then continue again a little further on.

Removing the map from its clear plastic case, I began wrestling with it, to get the thing folded over to show our present position, but mid-fold a forceful gust of wind wrenched it from my grip. As soon as it escaped my hand, the map assumed a graceful quality. The map was now free. My mother and I could only watch, mouths agape, as it danced in the air like a great white bird carrying our route – a green dashed line – in its clutches. It hovered over the edge of the precipice for an eternal moment then plunged downwards, gannet-like, into the abyss. There was no use in searching; we both understood that. At that moment my mother and I both knew where we were, but not what we were doing there.

We discussed our options. Retracing our steps would take a very long time and in this driving fug there was a very real likelihood of us getting lost in the maze of towers. We knew where the Witch's Step was, and our previous study of the map had suggested that on the other side was a relatively easy walk down a broad ridge back to the Datsun. So, we slung our rucksacks on our backs, walked to the edge and peered over the precipice.

The step was funnelling the wind-driven cloud through itself as if it were an hourglass but with vapour instead of sand. The week before, I'd seen *The Black Hole* at the Palais Cinema, with Maximilian Schell gazing awestruck into the void. 'A journey that begins where everything ends', ran the tagline.

Sitting on the edge, my mother gently lowered herself into a squeeze chimney with a grassy ledge about two body-lengths below. Beyond this was steep ground for about fifty body-lengths to the base of the notch. She slid down and I slid after her. Once I had joined my mother on this ledge, I began to feel a tightening nervousness in my chest. There was a problem that I couldn't yet fathom. Then I grasped it and the seriousness of our predicament dawned on me. That which we had so easily slid down we could not climb back up. My mother and I had inadvertently become committed to an unknown descent of a precipitous cliff. This was the first time in my life I had felt committed to something, anything, and it felt intensely real.

We continued our descent, clambering over ledges. I noticed peculiar scratches covering the rocks down our route. It didn't take too much insight to recognise these as crampon scratches. I was an avid reader of mountaineering books and had seen crampons in Chris Bonington's *Annapurna South Face*, borrowed from Bolton Library. I imagined what this place might look like in winter. Pictures of Don

Whillans in an orange one-piece down suit scratching along a rocky outcrop amid a sea of vertical ice abstracted my view. Suddenly I was in the high Himalaya. The scratch marks provided useful markers to keep us on the line of descent. I had not seen a pair of crampons at this point in my life but somehow these scratches validated our adventure.

When we finally completed our descent into the chasm, my mother perched on a gabbro boulder, buried her face in her cupped hands and began to weep. What were we doing here? Mum was no climber, and neither was I. She had a second-hand clothes stall on Farnworth market and was used to working hard to support us when Dad's property repair business was struggling. Or when he had taken off to Benidorm again, to sing Tom Jones and Sinatra covers in the English hotels for a little money. Family life seemed to get on top of him sometimes. He would hear 'Guantanamera' in his head and leave us in his purple velvet suit for the Costa Blanca and hopes of adventure.

For a moment I didn't know what to do with myself. I always felt uncomfortable when Mum wept: she didn't do it very often.

The wind was now siphoning through the narrow cleft and buffeting us powerfully. After a sip of sweet tea from our tartan flask, I scouted the terrain on the other side of the split. I could make out more scratches leading up a crack that ran through a small overhang at head height. I beckoned my mother over. She had composed herself again. The two of us inspected the problem. I attempted to clamber around the overlap but my new Hawkins Helvellyn boots kept skidding out of the crack.

My mother, raising her voice above the wind, shouted, 'Why don't you stand on my shoulders, love?' So, I climbed on her in my big boots and stood uneasily on her shoulders. This feat of amateur acrobatics allowed me to grasp a small ledge and I scrabbled my feet up the crack to gain the top of the first step. A couple of years later I learnt this move was a favourite technique of Eastern European sandstone climbers; it was known as 'Czech tech' or 'combined tactics'.

Now it was my mother's turn to climb up to me. I could not safely reach down to her and neither was I strong or heavy enough to make it a safe option if I could. Her hand would either have slid out of mine or Mum would have pulled me off my perch. I glanced down to her, then at the swirling mist to left and right. She knew, and I knew, that she had to do this on her own if we were going to get out of there.

So, my mother shut her eyes and opened them again in a very slow blink. She placed her right hand in the crack and her left on a depression by her shoulder in the slab of rock. And then, wedging her right boot in the crack, she heaved. To my young mind she was the epitome of composure, graceful in her movements, like a real climber. I waited nearly forty years to talk with her about that day and she told me that she was terrified, while knowing she could not show her distress for fear of alarming me.

'I thought we were going to die and that I was to blame,' she told me.

But somehow she made it to me and we climbed the rest of the step with relative ease. The remainder of the descent off the broad ridge of Caisteal Abhail was straightforward enough and when we reached a lower altitude the ferocious gusts finally ceased. From the ridge I could see the solitary sanctuary of our blue Datsun and in a seeming instant we were transported to our car.

In her Lancashire sparrow's voice my mum said, 'Well, that's the last time I'll be doing the Witch's Step.' And it was.

At an early age, certainly on the Witch's Step, I had an uneasy feeling all was not as it seemed. I sensed the incredible freedom of The Mountain, but could not put my finger on what exactly that freedom entailed. As I grew up a little, I learnt what freedom is not. I learnt that freedom certainly does not come from doing whatever you want to do, good or bad. And trust me, when I was a youth I attacked both with equal vigour, whether it be planting my own garden or setting the moors alight to watch from the heather as the fire engines arrived.

As a hunt-sabbing teenager, I understood freedom to be liberation from oppressive governments, and definitely from the ever-present risk of confinement by the justice system.³ As a young adult, I considered freedom to be what I found in wild nature, living as I chose, my body unfettered, my spirit unobstructed by expectation. Over the years it has become apparent to me that true freedom is none of these things. It's proved a slippery eel, and its real meaning to me has developed ever since the 'map incident' on the Isle of Arran.

I did not learn how to stick to a course until I was fourteen years old. Very much affected by the disintegration of my parents' marriage, I became one of those infamously wayward boys – arson was my speciality. And then, just a few short years after the Witch's Step experience, I had the good fortune to meet Harold Woolley, my physics teacher at Smithills School. He was a gangly bespectacled mantis of a man. Judging by the pronounced bow of his legs he had suffered from polio as a child.

Mr Woolley, as we had to call him, took me under his wing after I jumped over the banister of the fourth-floor physics laboratory. To this day I have trouble understanding why I did it.

I fell down the stairwell, accelerating as I went, grabbing at the steps and banisters of the lower floors. It had something to do with Mum and Dad … past the chemistry floor … I think I wanted to prove to them I could survive it … then mathematics … or maybe it was just for the rush … and finally geography. I landed hard on a radiator in the tiled basement of the swimming pool area, knocking myself unconscious. An ambulance was called.

After I came out of hospital, 'Woolley', as we actually called him, urged me to join the climbing group he was setting up. He began taking eight reasonably troubled boys to Wilton Quarries above Bolton. No girls were invited to come with us. It was the early 1980s and they had to play netball.

Wilton and the other Lancashire gritstone quarries supplied the stone that lined the reservoirs that powered the Industrial Revolution. The birth of the 'dark satanic mills' took place only spitting distance

---

3   I sabotaged fox hunts, which I believed to be immoral.

from Wilton. I was born in a gritstone house on the very top of the quarry. My brother and I had spent an earlier part of our childhood wandering the moors with .410 shotguns, learning how to make snares and night fishing in the 'lodges'.[4]

We lived so close to the quarry that I used to push chunks of our garden wall over the edge to hear the stones crash to the bottom. I had spent long heady days scrambling about down there, setting fire to the moors and throwing petrol bombs at climbers, so I had fond memories of Wilton. It came from a time when my mother and father were still happy together. Since the divorce, I had lived with my mum and sister in a cramped flat above a hairdresser's.

We all piled out of the school minibus below a luminous green gap up on the moor. Grey canvas rucksacks were passed out between us and we marched in file up the track towards it. Then we each upended the bags behind the rifle range, where the Bolton Gun Club came to practise. Dad and I used to go to this very spot to collect spent bullets. Then we would melt the lead down in an old saucepan and sell it to the scrapper man in town.

Next, Mr Woolley gave us instruction in the mysterious art of rock climbing. First, he showed us how to buckle the nylon belt and, like a sergeant major inspecting his men, he made sure we had also doubled them back.

Judd uncoiled the stiff eleven-millimetre rope at the foot of the cliff. Reeve checked out the metal hexcentric shapes, from tiny nuggets to things as big as cowbells. I fumbled with a large aluminium number '8'.

'We're going to climb up there,' said Mr Woolley, grinning and pointing a bony tarsus up at a dirty quarry face. 'It's called "Rappel Wall". All the climbs have their own names and difficulty rating,' he added.

It had been raining and the water had brought a film of damp grey talc over the top. It mingled with the green coating of lichen. We each clipped a heavy steel screw gate karabiner to our waist belts. Each boy was instructed to clip into this when it was his turn to climb.

---

4   Lodge: a Lancashire colloquialism for 'pond'.

Woolley then 'led' us boys up 'Rappel Wall'.

'The figure 8 is used for safety. You're going to belay me.'

He threaded the rope through the 8, 'Like so,' and clipped it to my belt.

'You're going to pay out the rope like so,' he mimicked the action, 'making sure not to pull me off. Okay?'

'Okay.'

I remember gazing up at him, impressed at how nimble he was. I had only seen him pacing up and down between the benches of the physics lab, occasionally reprimanding a naughty youth. Now here he was, Mr Woolley, his praying mantis body moving slowly to and fro, as if he was stalking some insect or small vertebrate. Then quickly he would pounce, grabbing a ledge and swinging up on to it.

'Can you see how I'm always keeping my weight over my legs so as not to knacker my arms too much?' he called down instructions to us. 'And you can sling a spike ... like ... so.'

How could an old man – he must have been at least fifty – be so agile?

Russ climbed. Then it was Dixon's turn. Now it was mine. I stepped up to the face. The rock was almost dry.

I knew these quarries like the back of my hand. Growing up, I had scrambled all over them, and later realised I had done some graded rock climbs, though without ropes and all the other paraphernalia. Later I learnt this was called 'soloing'. But now I stepped up on to the first ledge in my unbranded black gym shoes and grasped a chalky hold with my hand. Immediately all thought, except for the next move, left my head. The rock was steeper and substantially more difficult than the scrambles I used to do, and I was glad of the rope above me. I pulled on to a narrow shelf, my cheek in contact with the dirty face. I could smell the rock.

Then we climbed another, and another, and another.

I found I could execute gymnastic moves, when I was almost but not quite falling off the rock, in the knowledge that if I were to fall I would not be in any danger.

For a lad whose idea of a good time was getting drunk in the daytime and setting stuff alight, this was a revelation. I loved this new feeling but couldn't quite put my finger on what that feeling was exactly. Not yet. But up until that point I had never stopped still long enough to put my finger on anything. All I knew is that I had found something special.

Every week we piled into the minibus with Mr Woolley and I steadily became more proficient, distinguishing my jams from my finger locks, my mantelshelves from my rockovers. I also began visiting the quarry at weekends and sleeping in the heather. On waking up I would prime my brother's Optimus petrol stove, take a teabag out of my parka, fill my army surplus billy with water and descend into the hole.

By this time, I had a few bits of climbing kit and a new pair of injection-moulded EBs.[5] I had a circuit of solo climbs that I had 'wired' and would go up and down these ad nauseam.[6] I would wait for someone to climb with, though very soon I became part of a tight-knit community. It seemed like I had found my niche and, what's more, I was excelling at something for the first time in my life.

By a circuitous route, these first climbs opened the door to a life of travelling the world's wild places and climbing the world's mountains, and ultimately a life of freedom.

Years later, Noel Craine and I were fresh back from the first ascent of the west face of Mount Asgard on Baffin Island. We were giving a slideshow at the Bolton Aquarium and Mr Woolley – 'Call me Harold!' – introduced us. He was beaming and obviously very proud.

'I taught Paul everything he knows,' he began.

It is ironic that we find freedom on a mountain ridge or climbing a crack up a rock face, because these things confine us. We have to follow the line. We may have minor variations of choice, to use the same holds in a different sequence, or to climb the face for some

---

5   One of the first specialised rock-climbing boots, though not very good.
6   When done so many times that they were easy for me.

distance before returning to the crack. We may traverse on the left side of the ridge instead of the right. But essentially, once we set off on a route, we have to climb *that* route. We are committed to ascending *that* line. It is very much like the games of cricket I used to play in the ginnels of my youth.[7] One could hit the tennis ball to the left or right, but it was still destined to go towards the solitary fielder. The Mountain is like this. It dictates the line we take. And yet, despite that, the freedom The Mountain offers is vast, even limitless.

How can this be? This is the great paradox of The Mountain.

It is a paradox many mountaineers recognise, and one I first experienced on the Witch's Step. That experience was so profound that ever since I have harboured a keen interest in what constitutes freedom, reading books on the philosophy of freedom, from Rudolf Steiner's book of that name to Rousseau, Gandhi and the Romantics.

It is this same paradox, of constriction versus a kind of flight to the stars, which seems to draw parallels with the 'gambling' in the mountains that Samuel Taylor Coleridge undertook. His risk-taking behaviour with opiates is well documented, but he also had his dangerous adventures in the mountains. Decades after scrambling on Arran with my mum, I was reading *The Letters of Samuel Taylor Coleridge,* including one dated 8 August 1802 that is famous in English climbing lore. For me, it describes the first feat of mountaineering in Britain.

'The Scafell Letter' was written to Sara Hutchinson, William Wordsworth's sister-in-law and Coleridge's extra-marital love. In it Coleridge revealed a peculiar and, some might say, dangerous corner of his psyche, admitting to a sort of Russian roulette of the mountain variety. The poet describes how he committed himself to a descent of Broad Stand from the top of Scafell, a high Lakeland peak and the second highest in England. He could see the pass of Mickledore and the summit of Scafell Pike, the highest peak, beyond, but having skirted round precipices, found himself 'cut off' from what he judged to be

---

7   Ginnels: passageways in terraced houses in the UK used to access the backyard.

'a most sublime Crag-summit'. Instead of turning back and retracing his steps, Coleridge decided, 'relying upon fortune', to climb down anyway, whether or not it was even possible. By his own admission he was 'too confident and too indolent' to look around him to find a path or 'other symptom of safety'. He preferred to plough on despite the risks.

Coleridge descended 'with tolerable ease' until he came to a perpendicular rock face of about seven feet, which he clasped with his hands and dropped down. Onward and downward he went, dropping off a succession of these little vertical walls. But when he looked down to judge his route, Coleridge could only see more of the same and now began to suspect that he ought not go on. Now the poet discovered that while he could drop down a smooth wall of seven feet with ease, he could not make the climb to reverse it, and so he wrote, 'go on I must and on I went'. He continued down, with every drop bringing him closer to the rotting carcass of a 'crag-fast' sheep. With every drop the palsy of his limbs increased. He shook all over and joked, 'Heaven knows without the least influence of Fear.' There were only two more walls to drop now, but one of those smooth walls was twice Coleridge's own height. The ledge at the bottom was so 'exceedingly narrow', he noted to Sara, 'that if I dropt down upon it I must of necessity have fallen backwards and of course killed myself.' After my mother and I inadvertently committed ourselves in this way on the Witch's Step, I knew exactly how he felt.

In those weeks Samuel Taylor Coleridge spent in the Lakes, he was experimenting with freedom. He was paring away his avenues of choice, to a dangerous – though considered – degree, despite being so ill-equipped. Neither climbing rope nor ice axe was commonly used in Britain until the Victorian era. By committing himself to the descent of Broad Stand, with each irreversible drop, Coleridge was choosing not to choose. In doing so the poet had stumbled upon a paradoxical truth: the less choice we have, the freer we are.

As Coleridge's avenues of choice were stripped away, he became free from fear. He had transcended choice. For a brief moment he was floating above the material world. Coleridge – poet, preacher, addict – had become, if only for the duration of the descent, a 'self-actual-ised being', to use psychologist Kurt Goldstein's term, coined over a century later. It is this freedom that countless climbers instinctively search for when they engage with The Mountain.

Coleridge lay back on the ledge, his limbs trembling, and succumb-ed to a type of religious experience he had not experienced in church. He began laughing at himself like a madman:

> I lay in a state of almost prophetic Trance and Delight and blessed God aloud, for the powers of Reason and the Will, which remaining no Danger can overpower us! O God, I exclaimed aloud – how calm, how blessed am I now. I know not how to proceed, how to return, but I am calm and fearless and confident. If this Reality were a Dream, if I were asleep, what agonies had I suffered! what screams! When the Reason and the Will are away, what remain to us but Darkness and Dimness and a bewildering Shame, and Pain that is utterly Lord over us, or fantastic Pleasure, that draws the Soul along swimming through the air in many shapes, even as a Flight of Starlings in a Wind.

In this moment, the oft cited 'first climber for climbing's sake' touched on something vital. Lying on that ledge, the poet transcended the material world to join a cosmic dance, where the individual dissolves and becomes the universe. The one became all, and all became one. In that moment, he had become liberated from choice. Coleridge saw the ultimate nature of reality on that day.

Coleridge then observed that a section of the cliff face was 'rent from top to bottom': he had found an escape route, a chimney, and, measuring the breadth of the fissure, found that there was no danger of being wedged in, so he put his knapsack round to his side and slid down between the two walls without any danger or difficulty. The next drop brought him to safety.

Coleridge was coerced into descending that particular route by the route itself. He had no choice, just as the climber, once she or he steps off the ground, is coerced into ascending a certain sequence of holds by that sequence of holds. Once Coleridge embarked on his adventure, he wholly consigned his life to the will of The Mountain. In the process of surrendering to the descent, he held his destiny in his fingertips and as his contemporary William Blake wrote, 'infinity in the palm of [his] hand.'[8] He was truly free.

The pursuance of freedom *from* choice can and does lead to crucial discoveries about oneself, whereas freedom of choice quickly becomes a burden. Too many choices, as there frequently are, only lead us to confusion and regret for choices not taken.

The frustration of choice overload begins in the supermarket when we're confronted by over twenty types of toilet paper, or forty different cheeses. The soft drink aisle contains upwards of fifty different kinds of carbonated beverage: Pepsi Max™, Pepsi Free™, Pepsi Wild Cherry™, Pepsi Clear™, Pepsi AM™, Pepsi Fresh™, Pepsi X™, Pepsi Candy™, Pepsi Blue™, Pepsi Natural™, Pepsi Gold™, Pepsi Holiday Spice™, Pepsi Kona™, Christmas Pepsi™ (in the festive season), Lemon Pepsi™, Pepsi Lime™, Pepsi Mojito™, Pepsi Raging Razzberry™, Pepsi Strawberry Burst™, Pepsi Summer Mix™, Pepsi Freeze™, Pepsi Throwback™, Pepsi Tropical Chill™, Pepsi Twist™, Pepsi Vanilla™, Pepsi 100™, Pepsi Cherry™, Pepsi Cappuccino™, Pepsi Peach™, Pepsi Samba™.

And don't get me started on Coke.

Studies have shown that perusing a large number of fizzy drinks, or any other products in the supermarket, can impose a cognitive burden on us. In a famous experiment studying the effects of choice on contentment, Sheena Iyengar and Mark Lepper placed individuals into two groups. Group one had thirty types of chocolate to choose from, and group two had a choice of six types. Initially the larger choice group reported loving having the choice of thirty chocolates. However, they ended up feeling only dissatisfaction and regret about

---

8   William Blake, 'Auguries of Innocence'.

the choices they had made, imagining that they had chosen wrongly. Yet the cohort with the restricted choice reported increased satisfaction.

Clearly, too much choice is an unfortunate side effect of the consumerist world we find ourselves inhabiting. However, there is a way to experience real freedom. By engaging with wilderness, confronting fears, taking calculated risks, following The Mountain Path, we are constantly training and developing the neuroplasticity of our brains to accept change and adapt. American Barry Schwartz in *The Paradox of Choice* nails two detrimental effects of choice overload: regret avoidance and anticipated regret. Schwartz argues that the danger of all this choice is that it produces 'paralysis rather than liberation', although perhaps not the liberation Coleridge experienced on Broad Stand.

This problem was described as early as 1970, by the futurologists Alvin and Heidi Toffler, as a 'super-industrial dilemma'.[9] It pervades many aspects of our lives today. If we can experience regret by choosing the wrong chocolate or soda, how will we react to more serious decisions? Not simply which type of car we choose or the career path we map out, but our choice of lovers or life partners? The supermarket's marriage aisle is stacked with lots of different potential partners on its shelves. The consequence of too great a burden of choice is to make us less compassionate and more agitated, although I suspect many climbers and others who have immersed themselves in wild nature have always known this.

With limited choice there is less expectation of a positive outcome. We follow a particular sequence of holds up the cliff because it is the only thing we can do. We climb the ridge to the summit because it is the simple way. More choice brings greater expectation. Greater expectation leads to frustration and negativity.

It was not until I head-butted that rock in Tasmania and embarked on the process of becoming a member of the disabled community that I became truly aware that *real* freedom is in our heads, in the

9   *Future Shock*, 1970.

acceptance of our situation – any situation. Since crashing and almost burning on the Totem Pole I have taken this knowledge to every facet of my life and at least attempted to embody it. I eventually stopped wishing things wouldn't fall apart (excuse the double negative), and in doing so I stopped suffering when they did. And things do have a habit of falling apart.

Two and a half millennia ago, in northern India, a man named Siddhartha Gautama discovered this truth. Siddhartha, it is said, sat under a pipal tree and meditated for forty-nine days. Then it came to him in a blinding flash: all suffering is caused by craving. In the process of sitting there, Siddhartha became 'Buddha' (a Pali name which simply means 'awakened or enlightened one'). It's a popular story from the foundation of a philosophy that shared India's spiritual stage with Hinduism for a thousand years. Whether it is the desire for a better car or a craving for a different partner, the cessation of this craving leads to the cessation of suffering.

The austerities of a life led on The Mountain must also lead to a reduction in desires. Material pleasures on The Mountain are limited and few. We can't just pop down to the shops for some more milk or catch the latest movie at the cinema. We begin to crave less, and find that acceptance comes naturally. Once I had ceased craving for a miracle cure and accepted my situation as disabled, with little hope of climbing again, I *was* free. Not in some vague metaphorical sense, but really free. I could choose whether to suffer or not.

In this respect, we can be imprisoned by the trappings of a comfortable existence. However, we can also be bound by wild nature. If we hold craving in our minds, we can't escape suffering, whatever our environment. Conversely, it is possible to be truly free in prison or under an authoritarian regime. We can have our liberty although we may have a terminal illness or not enough to eat. We can be imprisoned by our own physicality – or lack of it, as I am. Or choose not to be. It simply takes mind training to create a different stance. I say 'simply', but the truth is there's nothing simple about it.

Most of us are encouraged to follow our dreams from childhood, but there are imposed limits to our dreaming. We are confined, often culturally, as to what those dreams can be. I wanted to be a train driver when I grew up, not a big-wall climber, not a writer. When the time came to leave school, I 'chose' a joinery apprenticeship. My other friends went into the army, secretarial work, policing or followed their families into various retail trades. One of my friends became a career criminal (to keep my police officer friend in a job). We become ruled by 'shoulds'.

We *should* go to school. We *should* go to university (actually, my father said I would never go to university if he had anything to do with it). We *should* be of a certain sexual orientation. We *should* get a good job, preferably high-paying so we can drive a big car and live in a posh house. We *should* pay into a pension fund. We *should* work until retirement. We *should* draw a generous pension. And, at the end of our life, we will expire, our blood will coagulate, our body's enzymes will autolyse our cells. We will desiccate and our minerals will return to the earth.

On the other hand, we *could* begin studying butterflies at the age of six. We *could* volunteer at a butterfly farm and become a distinguished lepidopterist. We *could* put off going to university or college and simply follow our passions. We *could* be of any sexual orientation we damn well choose. We *could* choose not to pay into a pension plan. We *could* never retire. We *could* draw pictures of butterflies. And, at the end of our life, we will expire, our bodies returning to their original constituents.

We have been conditioned from childhood to seek permission, not to seek freedom.

Aged seventeen I went on my first climbing trip, to Eryri and the mountains of North Wales. There could not have been a starker contrast than emerging from the Manchester smog and standing on a Welsh mountaintop. I could finally breathe. When I walked along the high street of Llanberis, I knew, right there and then, I had found my home. And when I ventured into the Padarn Lake Hotel, 'The Pad', I knew I had found my tribe.

A more colourful array of characters you never saw. A heady amalgam of young Welsh and English partiers who brought endless colour to the quarries' dark tunnels and holes with their raves … Welsh farmers and old ex-slate miners (the ones who had survived the ravages of silicosis) … Seedy drug dealers, hiding behind dense beards, shifting their eighths of squidgy black … Sharply dressed pill-pushers down from Manchester and Liverpool, plying their trade in five-quid disco biscuits right there in the pub. Throw into this volatile mix climbers living life like there was no tomorrow and you might get some idea of the intensity of this unique village. And yes, for some, sometimes, there was no tomorrow.

Then there were the young mums who always struggled to get someone to look after the kids, 'just for a couple of hours', the lively young shop assistants from the Co-op, the chemist and the Spar. It was the night they lived for, a high-energy but volatile mix. There were scuffles and fights all the time. On balmy nights these would spill out of the bar and into the Broccoli Garden, as we called the spliff smoking area out the side of The Pad.

The climbing scene in Llanberis in the 1980s was unique. Not just in Britain but the world. Fit young athletes were going out to the cliffs and mountains every day, mostly supported by Margaret Thatcher's GCG (Government Climbing Grant), as the dole was affectionately known in this former quarrying village. The Thatcher government had scattered people on the great spoil heaps of Dinorwig and completely forgotten them. But, out of the dark holes rose, phoenix-like, a ragtag army of climbers the likes of which Llanberis hadn't seen for a generation. As the unemployment figures rose, the trickle of climbers arriving in Llanberis became a mountain torrent. These climbers didn't give a stuff what anyone thought. They climbed blank faces as high as the tenement blocks from which many of them had come. They were bold, honest in their way, but also crazed.

In those days Llanberis had more than its fair share of precocious climbers, some bordering on genius. Johnny Dawes was the greatest, most naturally talented climber in the world in the 1980s. He never trained; he just went climbing. But how he climbed. To watch Johnny flow up a rock face was like watching a film of a tumbling stream of water, but in reverse. All the droplets conjured themselves together from a hidden place, pausing in one flowing cluster, and then powering upwards in a molten fountain. Yet, it wasn't just climbing that impelled Johnny. His head was filled with an intoxicating and often perplexing concoction of Buddhism, quantum physics, sexual partners and car racing. But it was the routes he climbed, both horrifying and gymnastic, that cemented his name in the history books.

Then there was Bob Drury, with a flair for wickedly thin rock faces. He was something special, I can tell you. Carlos had more than his fair share of strength and boldness. The Peng had a reputation for breaking people's legs but knew that real genius came through dedication to a cause. Moose, JR, Stickman, Manic, Big G, The Captain, The Wad, The Horn, The Stone, Tricky, Skeletor, Nicki, Manuel, Giant Redwood – they all had talent by the barrowload and could have made it big in the climbing world: whatever 'big' meant in those pre-internet days, before the #hashtag era. And yet, many of my peers suffered from brilliance gone wrong or curdled. Llanberis in that era had more flawed geniuses than you could shake a stick at.

Reality was either too simple or too much to bear for these unstable rock artists. They wanted to test the limits of life. They wanted to find something fantastic. Many found transcendence, if only for a moment, on the mountains and sea cliffs of North Wales. There were plenty of climbers who searched for the eternal in drugs; some in partying and dancing all night. Some searched for it through sex and promiscuity; yet others through criminal behaviour. I realise now we were all blindly searching for truth in our own way. And, some found the eternal, really found it, at the bottom of a cliff face.

I used to dream of being someone. If one of my friends made a climb, I would often be there to do the second ascent and make sure I told them how easy I found the moves. And I would always try and downgrade their creation if possible. 'That was never E8,' I once said to my great friend and rival Andy Pollitt. I had just made the second ascent of one of his major new additions at Gogarth on the Anglesey coast. *A Wreath of Deadly Nightshade*, he had named it.

'It was more like E5,' I added smugly.

He simply cast the deep black pools of his eyes upon me and I saw the disappointment in them.

'Oh, Paul,' those eyes seemed to say.

I remember a curious, heavy feeling in the pit of my stomach. Was it disappointment in the fact that his climb wasn't the latest 'hardest route in North Wales', or was it disappointment in myself? Surely the latter, although I didn't know it then. I had put down a mate for no reason. And it wasn't even true. He was always the greater climber.

By the time the climbers of Llanberis reached their thirties, many of them were either dead or damaged goods. Some made it through, and I count myself lucky to have survived those days. And I am content to have lived amongst this community of misfits for a few years. And anyway, as Jim Morrison said, 'No one here gets out alive.'

When I went to a mountain, I was very single-minded. You have to be so to succeed, or so I thought. I was a weird combination of self-absorbed athlete and thrill-seeker. Just as Coleridge's Ancient Mariner really couldn't put his finger on just why it was that he shot that albatross with his crossbow, so I had difficulty understanding the ramifications of my impulsive actions. Perhaps I took after my father, who shot a hovering kestrel out of the sky just for the hell of it. I just stood there. I was blind to the cause and effect of any given situation, whether I was shoplifting, imbibing drugs until I fell over or being responsible for my own safety while climbing a rock face.

So, one could say I found transcendence by trespass in that dangerous summer of 1986. I should not have been on the Red Walls of Gogarth that day, or indeed any other day, with such a turn of mind.

Gogarth is a complex series of frightening, white sea-cliffs. Perhaps a thousand rock climbs grace its folded zawns and cliffs. The Red

Walls are divided into Left-Hand and Right-Hand, separated by a noisy promontory, noisy because of the guillemots, razorbills and puffins that nest on its ledges. The Left-Hand Red Wall is a vertical desert of featureless quartzite, and back in the 1980s it had acres of unclimbed rock: scope for dangerous new climbs.

Weeks previously I had roped down Left-Hand Red Wall and hammered in a knife-blade piton, a peg that resembles a butter knife. This butter knife penetrated the rock less than an inch and sloped downwards from its crack, meaning it would pull out more easily. So I tied it off and carried on down the rope. Now, these small blades of steel are normally used on thin seams on the hardest artificial climbs, such as those on the huge cliffs of El Capitan in California's Yosemite Valley. But I was going to use this sliver of metal as a belay to hang on and fetch my partner up, along with some measly shards of brass on wire called RPs.

* * *

I arrive at the stance. I clip the tied-off peg and lace the rock with the four little splinters of dull-golden metal barely wider than a coin turned on its side. I arrange an equalising mass of shock cords and hang off the belay. There is one cigarette-packet-sized foothold on which to stand on the edge of this tilted desert. Bobby joins me and expresses his alarm at the inadequacy of the gear he is expected to hang off. I calm him down by letting him know I am very unlikely to fall off.

I lace my rock shoes and squeak the smooth rubber soles. I unclip from the belay and set off climbing. I attempt a rockover move with my left boot on a tiny nipple of quartz. I have to reverse this repeatedly. I am very nervous but think to myself, 'You can't let Bobby know you're terrified.'

Back at the hanging belay I look down. The sea is pounding the cliff seventy metres below us.

I squeak the rubber on the inside edge of my left shoe, climb up to the nipple move on its outside edge so as to keep the inside clean and consequently less likely to grease off. It holds. I pull through. I place a tiny wedge of aluminium, a Rock 1, in a thin crack. Up above I see no more protection. I climb on … I climb on … And on … I am fighting now to maintain contact with the rock. I think Bobby is shouting up words of encouragement.

I hear, 'Come on, Aardvark!' He calls me that because of my lengthy nose.

And then, the whole world turns a blinding white. I cease to struggle. Through a kind of fog or the frosted glass of a windowpane, I watch my body climb as I climb on. I hear the muffled cries of guillemots but from another place, outside of myself. Their screaming seems slow. I feel a grain of sand crushed to dust under the weighted edge of my shoe, but from where I'm watching myself. I smell the earthy odour of the lichen right in front of this man's face, though not through this man's nose. I watch myself with a supernatural detachment, executing move after move up the red rock.

And then I arrive at the clifftop, numb. I arrive at the right angle where my tilted world meets the horizontal. Another world, one of tourists and ice creams. A world I do not have much time for. I bring Bobby up on the rope and fail to mention my strange encounter with this other man called Paul.

* * *

I didn't know what I wanted in every other field of life. But I did know I wanted that feeling again. That feeling of sublimity. I searched for it. I looked high and low. At the top of The Mountain and in partying all night. The feeling seldom came, but I kept on searching. I did have other experiences of complete transcendence while climbing, but only a handful. And then they were gone. It was only after years of following this path, only after years on this treadmill of constantly reaching for and never quite grasping this intensely powerful feeling, that I realised something.

It didn't matter.

It didn't matter what I did. I could have done anything, been anything. Just as long as I was in wild nature and doing whatever it was to the best of my ability, that was enough. The presence, the feeling with which I did it was what I came to see as truly important.

One could say I was rescued by The Mountain. However, The Mountain is no escape. After all, it is often excruciating work, climbing a mountain. Exhausting work to keep going, knowing you could make it stop in an instant if you were to turn right around and slide back down the slope, or abseil down the rope. Climbing a mountain is dangerous work too.

One has to have discipline by the barrowload for all the austerity and hardship The Mountain provides. In the *Patala Sutta* ('The Bottomless Pit'), Gautama Buddha speaks of the mind's underlying habitual tendencies. He urges us 'not to be touched by painful bodily feelings.' For me, freedom comes with the acceptance of this pain. And the pain of hard work, though not in any regular nine-to-five sense.

A personal example would be my first big-wall climb, with my teammates Noel Craine, Sean Smith and Simon Yates. The year was 1991. We had chosen one of the world's most formidable peaks to make our multi-day first ascent, the Torre Centrale de Paine in Patagonia. At 1,200 metres the east face is several hundred metres taller than the Burj Khalifa in Dubai, the tallest building in the world. And we had spotted a hairline fracture running the entire height of it.

Noel and I had done numerous avant-garde climbs up the UK's most dangerous cliffs and we were to bring a touch of the avant-garde to the expedition. For Sean and Simon, with their long list of cutting-edge new routes up peaks in the Alps and the Himalaya, alpinism was their speciality. We were to meld the two styles together and attempt to work magic.

One week into the climb, storm-bound in the porta-ledge, I stared vacantly at my swollen hands.[10] I could hardly make two fists, so stiff

---

10 Porta-ledge: a cross between a hammock and a stretcher used for camping on multi-day wall climbs.

were they from days spent hammering pitons, or from attempting to jam my fingers into the thin crack we were following. Noel was slumped opposite me. I glanced up at him and it was in that moment I became aware my mind was being steadily shaped by all this time spent climbing among the great cliffs and mountains.

Following that thin seam, seemingly to infinity, with no avenue to venture left or right, it became clear that I was now pursuing *that* life. That life of a sustained freedom: freedom *from* choice, and from the shackles of convention. By rights, at the age of twenty-three I should have completed my joinery apprenticeship and gone on to a career in carpentry on various urban building sites. Yet here I was on the edge of this vast plain of granite, gingerly edging my way up, tapping pitons, like a cabinet maker taps a chisel, ever so delicately, to make one more move. Like a safe cracker, it would only take one mistake to set the alarms off, for the automatic steel vault door to lock shut, and I would fall for 'miles'. This was indeed how the climb, which we dubbed *El Regalo de Mwono* ended for Simon.[11] He fell one day into the void when a piece of protection ripped under his weight, a fall that left him bruised and shaken.

There was only one option for ascent, to continue climbing this dead-straight fissure, this hairline crack. There was only one other option: going down the same way we had come up. Going down is, most of the time, a lot easier than up, but down is always filled with regret; going up not so much. At least in this place, in that moment, I was not spoilt for choice. I was living the life I had been searching for, ever since the Witch's Step.

---

11   *El Regalo de Mwono* means 'The Gift of Mwono'. Mwono is a local Tuelche deity who is said to reside amongst these rock spires.

2

PILGRIMAGE

The cock crowing in the milky dawn thinks its call raises the sun; the child howling in a closed room thinks its cries cause the door to open. But the sun and the mother follow courses set by the laws of their own beings. Those who see us even though we cannot see them opened the door for us.

— René Daumal, *Mount Analogue*

It would be the dream start to our marriage. We would go bird-watching and golfing, take in the Great Wall and the Terracotta Warriors, and perhaps visit the Forbidden City. Carol Hurst and I were planning a honeymoon tour of China, memories of which would last a lifetime. Or at least, that's what we told China's National Immigration Department. The reality was different. We wanted to see whether two people with significant disabilities, those two disabled people being us, could cycle over a thousand kilometres from Lhasa in Tibet to Kathmandu in Nepal, via Everest.

The year was 2011, not long after the Tibetan uprising of 2008 (or the '3/14 riots' as they're referred to in the Chinese media, mimicking 9/11), when hundreds of Tibetans and Han Chinese died. Tibet had only recently been reopened and was still heavily restricted to foreigners. If we had so much as mentioned Tibet on our visa application, it would have been found in some consular office wastepaper basket. Yet it seemed it might be possible to purchase a Tibet permit once we were inside China. Two filmmakers, both old Tibet hands, Sharyn and Chris Jones, were travelling with us to record the ride for posterity. Of course, if we mentioned that we were making a film in Tibet, the consequences of that would no doubt be even more dire. *Filming* in Tibet – God forbid.

Back in Tasmania, Carol and I would take equal delight in each new map or guidebook the other had acquired. Together we had been attending night school and learning Pǔtōnghuà, Modern Standard Mandarin: the language spoken by the Han Chinese and also taught throughout Tibet. We had been informed this would be better than learning Tibetan because Tibetan has many dialects and, besides, everyone has to learn Pǔtōnghuà at school. For a year before our departure I carried Sam van Schaik's *Tibet: A History* and John Powers' *Introduction to Tibetan Buddhism* in my manbag. I had never thought much about Buddhism, or religion in general for that matter. I always considered myself a bit of a hedonist, but I had reached a point, due to my accident, where I was questioning everything and becoming increasingly interested in various philosophies and ethical standpoints.

When we arrived at Chengdu airport, Carol and I were taken aside and questioned at length on why we had brought these strange tricycles with us on honeymoon, and the two young border guards emphasised and re-emphasised that we were not to go anywhere near Tibet.

'No,' we told them, remembering to try out our Chinese: '*Bùkěnéng.* Impossible.'

Our ploy of telling barefaced lies to Chinese immigration seemed to work; Carol and I were soon Lhasa-bound on the highest railway in the world. Climbing up on to the Tibetan Plateau, the train groaned like a great monster and people were finding it difficult to breathe at over 5,000 metres. Chinese women and men queued for the oxygen masks placed in every sleeper carriage. Ibex, yak and wild ass dotted the plains. After two nights we disembarked at the vast hall of Lhasa station. Three fellow passengers were stretchered off our train suffering from altitude sickness.

In Lhasa we took our time acclimatising to the altitude and partied down at the legendary Nangma nightclub, where every self-respecting patron until recently carried a sword. Back on the rooftop of the Yak Hotel we breakfasted on boiled eggs, with unknown mountains on every horizon. In view of the Potala Palace we peeled the protective bubble wrap off our trikes and assembled the frames. I struggled to fit the disc brakes with my one good hand, so asked our filmmaker friend Sharyn for help. Along with her partner Chris, the party also included Mel, our physiotherapist, who was arriving from Canada.

We tested the trikes on a flat ride to Sera monastery on the outskirts of the city. The whole team was breathing hard in the thin air, but it was joyful to be spinning the pedals again. Approaching the monastery, I noticed elaborate murals painted on immense granite boulders strewn above the complex, in particular a blue demon stood on a wild ass lying on top of a person. In the car park several curious monks couldn't resist having a ride on our trikes. When it came time to go inside, we felt rather cruel locking them up and denying the monks some fun. But we couldn't risk the trikes getting damaged before we'd even set off.

Accompanying us inside the monastery was our guide, Samdrup, a guide being a requirement of the Chinese government for all foreign travellers in Tibet. The majority of guides in Tibet are Han and have limited first-hand knowledge of Tibetan culture or Buddhism, so we were lucky to secure an ethnic Tibetan to steer us through the country and its cultural mores. I would make great use of this luck in the coming weeks as I milked poor Samdrup for yet more knowledge. In fact, Samdrup means 'wish-fulfilling'.

As fit as he was, Samdrup could not be expected to cycle across the Tibetan Plateau and up to Everest. He required transport, accommodation and feeding. So we hired a truck and a driver, Mota, and a cook, Dawa. At first the whole-kitchen-sink approach to our adventure did not sit easily with me. But now that I am physically challenged, having a chair to put my shoe on, a table to eat off and a cook at the end of the day seemed rather practical.

We wandered through the massive rooms of Sera where giant colourful *thangkas* draped the walls: the white elephant entering Mayadevi's womb, Maya giving birth from her side to the future Buddha, images I recognised from my books.[1] There were pictures of animals of the forest approaching, like the nativity play I took part in every Christmas at primary school. I drifted in a daze, gazing at images: the tiger of ignorance, the bow of concentration, the arrow of wisdom, the wild elephant of the scattered mind. Starving Buddhas, meditating Buddhas, serene Buddhas ... Buddhas everywhere.

In another *thangka*, the great Diamond Mountain Range resembled the Himalaya on the horizon, and I could distinguish Meru with the four heavens floating above its summit (I was part of an expedition that attempted an earthly version of Meru in 1993, so I knew some of that mountain's cosmology). Another *thangka* described the hell realms: The Great Screaming, Pus and Blood, The Burst Blisters and Boiling Excrement.[2] Beings were trapped in a vicious but always finite suffering reminiscent of *The Garden of Earthly Delights* by Hieronymus Bosch, although the hell Hieronymus imagined was eternal. Evil Mara was depicted conjuring a host of demons turning themselves into beautiful women. These tempt Siddhartha Gautama, the yet-to-be Buddha, who sits seemingly oblivious. The demons throw spears and mountains at him, in an attempt to turn him to their sinful ways. Always Siddhartha sits in a half lotus, his hands in diverse postures.[3] And always there are paths, climbing into the mountains and sky.

In the Tamdrin Lakhang, the most sacred of Sera's chapels, Carol and I joined a long line of Tibetan pilgrims. We shuffled along the flagstone floor until we arrived at a shaven-headed monk. One after the

1   *Thangka*: a detailed scrolled painting used for meditational or instruction purposes. In English it means roughly 'recorded message'.
2   The hell realms are known as *Narakas* in Sanskrit.
3   *Mudra* in Sanskrit, *chakgya* in Tibetan.

other, he forced the two of us to our knees and thrust our heads through a wide crack. Both Carol and I, having mobility issues, struggle to kneel, so it must have appeared quite strange to the casual observer, as if the monk were wrestling with a couple of cripples, and coming out on top. Down I went until I was low enough to poke my head through the hole. On the other side was a shrine to Tamdrin, a peculiar horse-headed wrathful deity also known as Hayagriva, the protector of Sera. I strained painfully on my knees in the constricted space to kiss the deity's feet. I could only think of how he resembled Charley the crocodile from *Maisy Mouse,* a cartoon I used to watch with my kids.

The monk then painted our noses black with butter-lamp soot and Samdrup explained to him that we were riding all the way to Cho-molungma.[4] The monk nodded, muttered something to Samdrup, and positively beamed at us. He blessed us and draped a ceremonial *kada* scarf over each of our heads. Then we threw them on to the huge pile that was almost burying three particular Buddhas.

Afterwards, we passed an hour observing monks in their maroon robes debating in the courtyard. Sera monks are famous for these debates, which sometimes appear to get very heated. They debate philosophical points in order to increase their patience and wisdom, and therefore the patience and wisdom of the world. To me this made a lot of sense. For these Buddhist monks, society is not going to be improved by laws and government edicts, but by the individual search for, and understanding of, the *dharma*.[5] One of the ways to do this is by using logic to determine truth. In the Mahayana tradition, which includes Tibetan Buddhism, the focus is on attaining Buddhahood for the benefit of all sentient beings, practising *pāramitās* or 'supreme virtues' to become a *bodhisattva*. These virtues include meditation practice and adherence to a strict moral code called the *sila* that also applies to the lay community. The *sila* is all about the five precepts of

---

4   Chomolungma is the Tibetan name for Everest, with a similar Sinicised spelling Qomolangma.

5   The *dharma* is both the true nature of the universe and the practice of Buddhism.

abstinence: refraining from killing, stealing, lying, becoming intoxicated and sexual misconduct. Morally uplifted, Carol and I cycled
back to Lhasa.

Next morning we prepared to leave Lhasa and while posing for
photographs below the Potala Palace, a pre-pubescent soldier with an
ancient-looking rifle approached us nervously. He wanted us to know
that the prayer flags festooning our trikes were a highly dangerous
symbol and banned anywhere in sight of the Dalai Lama's former
residence. Uniformed snipers positioned on rooftops surrounding
the Jokhang temple in the centre of Lhasa had been a stark reminder
of the 2008 riots. One was studying us through his telescopic gunsight
from a roof at the north side of the square as we departed Lhasa on
the Beijing West Road to begin our journey.

On the edge of the city we passed a huge golden yak and, further
along, stopped at a ten-metre Buddha which, according to the woman
who cared for the site, had magically appeared in the rock face not too
many centuries ago. At camp that evening, I wallowed in the peaceful
waters of the Kyi Chu, oblivious to the thundering cement trucks
passing close to our tents. Chinese railway workers were busy building
the Lhasa to Shigatse extension line. The women were playing badminton with Samdrup and invited me to play, but I could not risk a
fall on day one of our ride, so declined their offer. Now I am disabled,
I have to choose my non-essential pastimes with added care. It's a
dangerous game, badminton.

Our Tibetan crew formed the idea that we were on a sort of pilgrimage, just like the many other pilgrims we had seen with wooden
paddles on their hands. They were prostrating their way slowly and
painfully to the holiest mountain in the Himalaya, Mount Kailash.[6]
The pilgrims, dressed in leather aprons to protect their clothes, would
lie face down, nose to the bare earth, or increasingly these days,
bitumen. They stretched their arms above their heads, raised the

---

6   Mount Kailash in western Tibet is sacred for Buddhists and Hindus alike, as well as for
     followers of Bon and Jainism.

wooden paddles on their hands from the elbow and placed them reverently together. The pilgrims then did a push-up and rose to their knees and then their feet, clacked their paddles above their heads, the fifth position in ballet, once more in front of their face, and once again in front of their chests, all the while muttering mantras, before stepping forward a body's length and repeating the whole process. Some pilgrims were dressed in rags, with braided hair, assorted headgear, the toes of their shoes repaired with pieces of car tyres, their foreheads callused from touching the road perhaps a thousand times a day. It can take seven months in this manner to prostrate oneself to Kailash.

We were heading slowly towards our own Kailash. If we cycled all the way to Chomolungma, me with half a body and Carol with chronic arthritis, covering a thousand kilometres over six huge passes, we would go some way to experiencing what these pilgrims endured: the deprivation, the focus, the pain and the strenuousness of it all. But why was pilgrimage to a mountain so important to the Tibetans? Why is pilgrimage important to anyone? All I knew was that the journey to Everest was important to me, but for reasons I did not understand or had simply not analysed.

Later that day Samdrup asked me a question in a sand quarry below an abandoned *dzong*.[7]

'Why do you make such a difficult pilgrimage?'

'We aren't on a pilgrimage,' was my slightly sharp response. I felt a momentary pang of regret. I was coming to value Samdrup's sharp observations and caring nature.

'Of course you are,' he replied.

I had previously thought little about pilgrimage. On expedition to Gangotri in India, I had seen Indians prostrating themselves towards Gaumukh, the cow's mouth, source of the Ganges, but simply considered pilgrimage to be something religious people did. I respected them for the hardship they were enduring for an ideal, but couldn't – or, more to the point, didn't want to – understand it. I was there for

---

7   A *dzong* is a fortified Tibetan monastic complex.

a reason, to climb a mountain, and nothing was going to sway my resolve. Here on the plateau it was hard to avoid the hundreds of pilgrims forcing themselves onwards in extreme discomfort.

'And, Samdrup, where are they going?' I already knew they were heading to Mount Kailash, but wanted to hear the importance of this particular pilgrimage from the beginning.

'They go to Kailash so that they can obtain good fortune.'

'I think I understand wanting to go on pilgrimage to a sacred mountain. To prostrate yourself for a thousand miles shows deep devotion.'

'Yes, devotion is there. But the good fortune I speak of is nothing material. It is mental training in hardship until we transcend pain.'

I understood that. I waited for more.

'It humbles a person going through so much hardship.'

'Ah,' I said. I had had my fair share of physical hardship, and if it taught me anything it was humility. The physical hardship of moving through this mountain landscape must stimulate an intense investigation of the landscape within. It can't do anything else. I, like the pilgrims, had been forced to face this investigation. And I had come to my own conclusions.

While in pain, I had been transported to another world. I had experienced things I couldn't quite understand. However, one thing I had learnt was to be present every single day, taking nothing for granted, especially one's health, and I became grateful for every event that befell me, both good and bad.

'I think I understand, Samdrup.'

'These pilgrims must have commitment and discipline,' Samdrup continued.

'I see. So, the process itself is the good fortune?'

'Yes, it is a transformative experience.'

'Well, this is why we ride to Chomolungma, to make the most out of our life, and in the process transform ourselves.' I continued my sentence in my own head, 'or at least to transform myself – I can't speak for Carol.' Then I said aloud, 'It is very similar.'

'However, Paul, one important thing.' Samdrup put his hand to his heart. 'Besides humility, we learn gratitude as a pilgrim. The pilgrim has nothing and must accept everything.'

I nodded in agreement. I had had to learn to accept help by the shovelful since becoming disabled. So much so that I had built my whole philosophy of life on acceptance.

'Finally, the possibility of loss, for the dangers are many on pilgrimage. Pilgrimage teaches us how to die with grace.'

'Wow,' was all I could manage, though I was thoroughly impressed.

'When a pilgrim dies on the road, it is never considered a pity. It is a great honour to leave the earthly shell behind while on the path to Kailash.'

My thoughts drifted to the scores of friends who have died in the mountains and how, generally, the climbing community is very accepting of it. Only now did I begin to understand.

I had always considered climbing to be a sort of grail quest, where one goes to a foreign land and struggles upwards to attain a summit and, once bagged, takes it home to add to the collection. Was the ultimate aim of riding to Everest Base Camp really to add another adventure to my collection? The further I travelled through the rarefied air of Tibet, the more uncertain my footing became. The further I cycled, the more my mind was being re-shaped. It was not a wholly disagreeable feeling.

Samdrup doodled six symbols in the sand: 'Om … ma-ni … pad-me … and … hum.'

The flat-topped letters of the Tibetan script dripped down to points below, almost as if the English alphabet were handwritten and turned on its head.

'That's beautiful, Samdrup.'

'This is the mantra of Avalokiteshvara, the Buddha of compassion, whose earthly embodiment is the Dalai Lama.'

Like just about everyone, I recognised the words but not the text.

'And here again in Sanskrit.' He first drew a horizontal line and then swirling figures underneath it.

'Om mani padme hum. This is what the pilgrims chant with every prostration.'

'What does it actually mean?' Carol asked, as she struggled to sit on the ground.

'The jewel in the lotus,' I piped up, showing off my newfound knowledge from all the books I had been reading.

'Well, Paul, it is more complicated than that. Very complicated, in fact.' Samdrup pointed to the first squiggle.

'The six syllables correspond to the six *pāramitās*,' he said and moved his finger rightwards, rattling them off in a well-practised list: 'Dana, Sila, Ksanti, Virya, Dhyana, Prajna.'

Then he said, '*Pāramitā* means "perfection". Every time you chant this mantra, you do so in a spirit of generosity, morality, patience, diligence and … ' – our guide paused the rightward drift of his finger on the Sanskrit as he called to mind the last two translations – 'concentration and insight. That's it.' He beamed proudly at himself for having accurately translated the six perfections.

'There is a lot more, including the six Samsaric realms, but this is too much for one lesson,' said Samdrup with a mischievous laugh.

At Chushul we met the waters of the Yarlung Tsangpo, which becomes the great Brahmaputra after it curls round the Himalaya. As we rode beside the river, the scenery became grander and more serene, but often I lost sight of Carol in the dust. That day we rode fifty-three kilometres, seventeen further than she had ridden since wholly succumbing to osteoarthritis in her mid-twenties. Carol had been a keen adventurer before her hips began rapidly to degrade. As avenues for outdoor activity narrowed, she took to white-water padd-ling with gusto, becoming a six-time Australian champion. Now she walked with a pronounced limp and used a stick. Her hips are not supple enough to use full-length cranks on a bike, but a specially customised trike with tiny pedal cranks would allow her to race up passes in Tibet.

We entered a narrow gorge where there were objective dangers aplenty: loose boulders overhanging the road, big concrete trucks thundering past and yaks precariously perched on clifftops. On one downhill stretch we passed a coachload of monks who had stopped by the side of the road. They all descended from the vehicle and, with a fervour normally reserved for rock stars, they waved, danced and cheered us on. Our trikes commanded so much attention that at one point on the road to Everest we caused a traffic jam as Chinese tourists queued for a photo with us.

As we exited the gorge, a huge Tibetan mastiff began chasing me. I tried to speed up, but at close to 4,000 metres I only left myself gasping like a landed fish. Thanks to my prone position I found myself face to face with the vicious creature. I could have sworn it slobbered on my chest. All I could do was offer my spastic arm to the angry beast as though it were a rubber chicken. Just as the monster was about to gnaw on my arm, Sharyn came to my rescue, charging the dog and frightening it off with a fierce growl.

A little further along, I approached a family of four dressed in rags, two with the hallmark butcher's aprons and wooden paddles of pilgrims: a father and young daughter. The mother was wearing a cowboy hat and had a blanket tied around her waist. She had a baby slung to her back, so was presumably excused from prostration duties.

I slowed to a halt. '*Tashi delek*,' I said using the Tibetan greeting in my phrasebook but pronouncing, unnecessarily, the hard 'k'.

The family paused their ever-forward momentum. '*Deley*,' replied the father laconically. So fissured was his face from the high-altitude sun that it seemed to map the whole Himalaya. I shared some chocolate with them, the daughter taking less than the parents, and after a comfortable silence, went on my way.

Glancing repeatedly at the pilgrims in my cracked mirror, I thought about their lives as my pedals turned monotonously. They worked laboriously, endured great discomforts and faced very real and ever-present dangers on the road to their *temenos*, their holy sanctuary. A surge of jealousy welled up in me. This family seemed to be living a real life, fronting up to real dangers: disease, hunger, hypothermia, and all for something they believed so much that it was worth risking their very lives. Those lives had a course, a trajectory, a meaning: the *dharma*. On the other hand, I chose these adventures, these expeditions, these stunts, because I could. Because I was lucky enough to have been born in a wealthy country.

'Is this all an extravagance?' I asked myself. This journey, was it simply an indulgence?

Though some of the pilgrims were just as impressed by our disabled journey as we were with their travails, I could not refrain from asking myself, 'Just what exactly is it that gives my life meaning?'

I knew climbing had given me a reason to live. And when it had been brutally taken away from me, I had been thrust into darkness for years. But why *was* climbing so important to me?

I thought about the act of creating a new climb. Like the ephemeral sand mandalas that Tibetan Buddhist monks spend days and weeks creating, the original performance can only take place once. Experience as change and transience. As we climb something that has never been climbed, we are enmeshed in a creative journey. Like 'process art', the journey is part of the creation and can only take place once. A climber making the second ascent will have the knowledge that it's been done before and will do it differently. Nothing is static. This is the nature of all things.

After a week of riding, we took our first rest day at a vocational farm near Shigatse called Braille Without Borders. Paul Kronenberg, one of the founders, told us stories of how some blind children are locked away through shame on the part of their parents. To be born blind in Tibetan culture, you must have done something terrible in a previous life. I recalled people's reactions to me while limping around Lhasa's streets. There was the odd scowl, one gasp of horror, and one person even spat at me. Any kind of disability is viewed in such a way in Tibetan culture. Paul, his blind partner Sabriye Tenberken and their team were challenging this ignorance about disability across Tibet and China. By cycling across Tibet, Carol and I were challenging ignorance of a similar kind at home.

Shortly after leaving Shigatse it began pouring with rain, which on a recumbent trike is a special kind of treat. We got soaked, and darkness was falling. Just as our band was beginning to contemplate spending the night out, Samdrup sped ahead to ask at a monastery if we could sleep there. The monks were quite reticent about allowing foreigners in, as it is illegal under Chinese law, but there was a lone monk at the gate to welcome us in from a spirit of generosity.

Carol and I passed through the gate and into a high-walled court-yard. I found myself shivering in time to each bump across the rough cobbles. Then Carol helped me stand and we dried ourselves off with towels passed to us by a tall monk. We introduced ourselves, but as so often happened I never quite got his name. Thanks to that ill-fated rock landing on my head, I often forget names and facts instantly (this is my key to living in the moment). Unusually the monk didn't seem at all fazed by Carol's limp and my demi-functioning body; he didn't mention it, anyway. The monk with no name informed us the other monks were in meditation in the hall.

We ate a cobbled together meal of thukpa soup with instant noodles in the monastery dining room.

'So, you are headed for Chomolungma?' asked the monk in excellent English.

Samdrup had already told him.

After some chit-chat about the likelihood of rain next day and the route we should take, I placed my empty bowl on the table. My mind drifted off, as it often does after a long day of riding. The conversation attained a far-away quality as my eyes scanned the walls.

A *thangka* featuring the Buddha hung above the table opposite where I was seated. The Buddha sat below a pipal tree in the lotus position with the soles of his feet upturned. His hair was in a topknot and a halo encircled his head. Five bald disciples were gazing up at him; a deer sat by one of them. In the background was a whole herd of deer. It was reminiscent of the stained-glass windows depicting the lives of the saints that lined 'The Iron Church' on Blackburn Road in Bolton, the Lancashire mill town I grew up in. I used to gaze at them, suitably awestruck, each Sunday: Saint Peter, Saint Paul, winged angels, with my own mantra, 'Holy, Holy, Holy'. I can still see the vitreous words fired on to the glass: 'He is not here; he is risen, just as he said. Come, see the place where the Lord lay.'

Last I heard they were going to turn it into an Italian restaurant.

'Can you tell me, what does the painting show?' I enquired of the monk.

'Well,' he cleared his throat, 'that is Lord Buddha delivering the first turning of the wheel of *dharma* to those,' his finger swept between the figures, 'his five followers.'

I nodded in acknowledgement.

'The first discourse was "The Four Noble Truths".'

I already knew the Four Truths. It's Buddhism 101: that life is made up of suffering, that craving or desire is the origin of suffering, that one can be free from suffering and the truth of the eightfold path which leads to the cessation of suffering.

'It is all contained in the Tripitaka,' said the monk with no name.

I had read about the Tripitaka in my *Introduction to Tibetan Buddhism*, as important to a Buddhist as the Bible is to a Christian.

'The Dharmapada says: "Of all the truths, the Four Noble Truths are the best; of all things, passionlessness is the best."'

'Passionlessness?' I felt my pulse quicken. To me, passion was a good thing. How could we live without being passionate? I thought of myself as full of passion. I had a passion for mountains, a passion for climbing, a passion for life. And when climbing was taken away from me, I collapsed in a heap with, wait a minute, a severe depression.

'Oh no,' I thought. My views were being turned on their head, yet again.

'I can see by your face you are confused.'

'So, *this* is what Buddhists mean by the Middle Way?'

Without me having to expand on this obvious paradox he went on, 'You can still bring your passion into life just as long as you do not become attached to it. This is what the Buddha means when he steers us away from our passions. Or else you would become reactive, hating people for what they have done, or clinging to impermanent things and suffering when they are lost to us.'

'Then a Buddhist can't be ambitious, right?'

'No. Ambition for what? To what end?'

'Most people, where I come from at least, are very goal-driven. I was a climber ... before my accident.'

I thought for a moment how to express the competitive streak in some of the climbers and mountaineers I knew.

'And climbers are some of the most driven people I know. They have numbers for difficulty, and the higher the number you can climb, the more fame you have.'

'Striving for perfection is a good thing,' explained the monk, 'but not at the expense of someone else, certainly not for fame. One has to be humble.'

There was a period of silence. I looked around the dining room. Every inch of the wood panelling was painted. Even the ceiling was painted with exquisite scenes in garish colours. More *thangkas*; a curtain displaying an endless knot covered a doorway leading to the kitchen. My head swam with fatigue. For a moment I was in the House of Fun at Blackpool Pleasure Beach.

The monk broke the silence with a carefully pronounced 'Chomo-lungma', before uttering a long guttural 'Mmmm.'

'Yes,' I answered, not really knowing if it was a question.

'The best teaching is one that reveals our hidden faults.'

His response seemed a little cryptic. Whatever did he mean?

'Yes, we are cycling all the way to Chomolungma,' I added just to make sure we were on the same page.

'Only when you are free from hope is the mind truly untroubled.' Did he hear correctly? The monk's command of English was excellent, but it seemed he was being deliberately obtuse. Was he on to us? Was that it? All this nonsense about getting to Everest Base Camp?

'And only the humble person remains without fear.'

Now I was becoming agitated. The monk seemed to be seeing right through me. He had taken aim and struck a raw nerve. I had long struggled with humility and was confused as to whether it was a good thing or a bad thing.

This question had been burning in my mind during those long hours in the saddle. I had been brought up a churchgoing Christian, taught from an early age that humility was one of the most important virtues a Christian could have. I was taught that 'God opposes the proud and shows favour to the humble.'[8] Conversely, some climbers I know think humility to be pretentious at best. I recall asking one of my climbing partners if he'd read a certain classic mountaineering book. 'I'm too busy writing climbing history to read it,' was his reply.

Indeed, humility has attracted negative connotations for the past few hundred years. Hume thought it a 'disagreeable passion' and Nietzsche believed it enshrined a 'slave morality'. Ayn Rand, in the guise of John Galt, her character in *Atlas Shrugged*, urges us to, 'Discard the protective rags of that vice which you called a virtue: humility.' It is said that humility creates followers rather than leaders, and that it is weak or cowardly to be humble.

However, it wasn't that sort of false or self-deprecating humility the monk was talking about. Rather, I think he meant having a sense of our true place in the universe.

My head was jerking from exhaustion and my eyes were starting to close. I apologised and offered my goodnights, knowing that our conversation hadn't reached a satisfactory conclusion. Shuffling over to the corner, I climbed into my sleeping bag and slept the sleep of the righteous on the rough floorboards.

After breakfast with the young monks, we tackled the Tra La, which at 3,975 metres is only a baby pass, and set up camp in a quint-essentially Tibetan landscape – flat plains with yaks and a view of

---

8   James 4:6

distant mountains. The setting sun was so beautiful, even against the silhouetted electricity pylons.

On the following day, when Carol and I were supposed to be playing a round of golf at Mission Hills Shenzhen, we found ourselves instead grinding painfully up the Gyatso La. At 5,220 metres, this was the highest pass of our journey and we needed to climb it over two days. The second day began with ruthless cold. My lungs were silently screaming as I tried to keep up with Mel, our physiotherapist and unintended pacesetter. Carol had to stop every kilometre to massage her deadened feet (due to decreased circulation). We pedalled slowly on past nomads living in yak-hair tents, like they have done for millennia, and, after two interminable hours, we surfaced into sunlight.

On the summit of the Gyatso La we were able, for the first time on our ride, to witness the vast wall of the Himalaya. I had awoken tired and jaded, so it was good to know we were inching that bit closer to our goal. (Well, my goal. The aim of the ride for Carol was not to reach Chomolungma but to complete the journey to Kathmandu.) Cho Oyu, sixth-highest mountain in the world, was lit up in the morning sun and I followed its east ridge across to the daunting block of Gyachung Kang, hardly less tall. Back in a previous life, after hearing of my Slovenian friend Marko Prezelj's climb of Gyachung Kang's north face, I had developed an urge to climb this mountain. As the fifteenth-highest mountain in the world and just missing out on the magic height of 8,000 metres, it is far quieter and cheaper than the fourteen '8,000ers'. And now? It appeared a frightful proposition.

My eyes drifted leftwards. To Makalu. Ever since borrowing Lionel Terray's *Conquistadors of the Useless*, which documented the French superstar's first ascent of the mountain, I'd had a pipe dream of climbing this, more than any other 8,000-metre peak. My dreams of a similar life in the mountains were crumbling and being swiftly rebuilt that freezing morning on the Gyatso La. Because there, standing before me, between Cho Oyu and Makalu, was Everest itself: Chomolungma. And I – we – were going to cycle all the way to that vast wedge. Although not before pedalling up and free-wheeling down several more 5,000-metre passes. Chomolungma's north face, still in shade at this time in the morning, was in stark contrast to the sunlit east face of Lhotse, squatting just behind it like a frosted cake. Carol added a prayer flag for her mother and I added two, one yellow, one red, for Cadi and Eli, my children. Then we rolled off down the pass.

After Shekar, we put in a sixty-kilometre day, with ten of those kilometres into a brutal headwind. Well, it was for me, with only half a functioning body. I was exhausted when I went to bed but woke at midnight with a strange feeling, an aura, and the familiar taste of metal in my mouth. My right arm was already beginning to flex when I came to, but began contracting painfully, uncontrollably. My hand started clawing like the chicken's feet I used to play with as a kid in Spain. I would pull on the tendons dangling out of the hacked shin. I attempted to call out, but no words came. It was all very distressing. I was used to epileptic fits but not in such a serious situation – in a tent in a remote part of the Tibetan Plateau.

I had not had a fit for five years. Even though I had been taking my anticonvulsant medication every day, my carbamazepine level had clearly been dwindling. This might have been because of the altitude, but was more likely due to the excessive exercise and strenuous breathing I was maintaining day after day. I vowed to make enquiries on my return home, and did, but no doctor knew the answer. It seemed I was probing a new frontier in the drug's capabilities. One thing I did know: just like the prostrating pilgrims, I was sustained by my own suffering.

The following evening, we reached the crux of our journey. Carol and I had been forewarned about the Pang La, a mountain road of 117 switchbacks to the pass at 5,200 metres. It's known to cyclists as the 'Pain La'. Huge Chinese slogans on the mountainside informed us of I don't know what. They might as well have been telling us that the following day would be impossible. Even Samdrup, who was supposed to be on our side, shook his head saying, 'How can two people with such disabilities tackle such a hill?'

I knew it shouldn't have, but his lack of faith in us sowed a seed of doubt at the back of my mind. He had been so supportive of our struggles up other high passes. I think, after twenty-one days on the road, he was becoming weary, like the rest of us.

I could see that this pass, the Pang La, was going to be the hardest point in the whole Lhasa-to-Everest journey, but I still made a twenty-yuan bet with Samdrup that Carol and I would ride up this hill. Sharyn, who had done the pass several times before, albeit in a truck, had faith in us, but even she recalled grown men weeping on the side of the road amidst thick clouds of dust. I stifled a shiver. We were going to attempt to ride over this mountain of dirt at dawn. As the sun set, the silhouette of a crumbling fortress poised high on an outcrop of rock dominated the broadening night.

We arose in the dark. Ice crystals sparkled on the tent fly as we ate breakfast. I joked into the camera that 'we're having a fun day at Shanghai Disneyland, and I'm really looking forward to riding on Space Mountain'.

We began at first light. The hot water we put into our bottles quickly froze. By eight o'clock we were at hairpin nineteen and a motorist stopped her car and offered us hard-boiled eggs. She watched us eat one each and made sure I ate another before getting back into her little car. Carol pulled away from me, her tiny pedal cranks going ten to the dozen as I sang Woody Guthrie's 'Dust Pneumonia Blues' out loud. The road was heavily corrugated, caused by the 'washboard' effect of the frequent trucks and buses. Yet this didn't seem to trouble us as much as the loose rocks and soft sand that cause wheels to spin tiresomely. This led to many stationary moments of gasping and wishing I had bottled oxygen like so many Everest climbers. We were pedalling back and forth up a scree slope and at times the prayer flags on Carol's flagpole were all I could see of her in the distance, above the rocks. Snow flurries began as we neared the top of the pass, which *only* had forty-six hairpins. A hundred and seventeen was to include our descent, thankfully.

Carol and I summited the Pang La in cloud together, through the usual tunnel of prayer flags. Passengers in the cars were scattering 'wind horses' printed on paper, their Buddhist prayers swirling in the sky. After a brief rest and a nibble on some dried fruit, I studied the descent. An endless knot of switchbacks which only Dr Seuss could have dreamt up: straight out of *Green Eggs and Ham*. Although obscured by the swirling mist, Chomolungma made its presence felt. I didn't hold back on the speed, but it felt as though I was going to get thrown out of my seat with every pothole my wheels disappeared into. Sharyn was waiting at the next village to record my thoughts on film even before I could climb off my trike. I told her, 'I feel like my internal organs have been put through a blender.'

Carol and I had the mountain in our sights, and nothing was going to stop us, although pedalling to Everest Base Camp the following day proved a gruelling exercise: uphill and all of it on dirt. We were forced to inhale clouds of dust put up by army trucks. Chinese people parked their four-wheel drives haphazardly by the barriers and shook our hands as we cycled past. Of course, me only having one hand meant that sometimes I almost crashed into them.

Just a few short kilometres from Everest Base Camp, we paused at Rongbuk monastery. I had dreamt of visiting this, the highest monastery in the world, ever since I was a kid. My Uncle Tom had visited Everest and this astonishing fact had become family lore. I recall him being a giant in stature and looking like Edmund Hillary. I was also reading *Tintin in Tibet* around that time, when Tintin and his terrier Snowy cross the Himalaya and are invited into a Tibetan monastery, which looked very much like the one I was seeing now. I think that in my young mind I merged all the stories together and had Uncle Tom making the first ascent of Everest and visiting Rongbuk monastery on the way.

Huge piles of mani stones and a great stupa marked the entrance to the monastery. The stupa was festooned with multicoloured prayer flags. These flags reminded me of bunting from the Queen's silver jubilee in 1977, when I was a kid, but without Elizabeth's head on every flag. I hobbled into the courtyard, using my spastic arm for balance as though tightrope-walking, and climbed the stone steps. The others were waiting for me in the simple structure as I took my cleated shoes off. We entered a small room, much like my Aunt Ada's living room but with colourful Buddha wallpaper instead of orange flock damask. Add a dresser painted gold and the match was pretty close. We listened to the monks playing horns and banging drums, and made a donation before we left.

I was realising a lifetime aspiration in experiencing the goddess mountain close up. The blinding Himalayan light, the sparkling light I swear I could hear, the rushing of the stream falling from the Rongbuk glacier, the texture of the granite and limestone glacier pebbles, much the same as river pebbles one might find lower down in a river. These smooth rocks at the very source of the Rongbuk river are ground down by thousands of years under the ice. I added two more cairns to the hundreds built by the tourists and pilgrims, like little chortens.

Chomolungma shimmered in the haze. From the north the summit rises three and a half kilometres vertically above base camp. I had to goose my neck to gaze up at the mountain's zenith from below my Tibetan Stetson. For thirteen years since the accident, I had spent every day learning to walk and talk again. When I was first recovering, I never thought I'd be able to travel again, never mind pedal all the way to the highest mountain on Earth. It had been a long and tortuous road getting here. From the first ride on my trike, everything I had done had been to get me here, to this place, today. I saw this clearly now. This was my pilgrimage.

However, as with any summit, the climb is only half the journey. There is often a relaxing of the guard that can make the return fraught with difficulty and danger, so Carol and I had to be vigilant still. Half a day down the valley from Everest we deviated from the main route where a sandy single track led us to the Nam La. We were well acclimatised by then, and so its 5,100-metre summit did not pose a problem from its altitude, but I still had to weigh my panniers down with rocks to prevent the rear wheel spinning in the sand.

In fact, the road was so rough that as we rode below Cho Oyu, I sheared a quick-release pin under my seat. We had no spare, so I had to accept Mel's and Chris's help as they lashed the seat back to the frame with a tyre inner tube. On the final stretch down to the sealed road, a kid threw a pebble at Sharyn's head with remarkable accuracy. She bled and hurled abuse at the diminutive troublemaker, but she was okay. After eight days of potholes, I kissed the metalled road surface.

On the last pass, the Lung La, we struggled into a headwind. The back of my knee hurt like hell. Mel came to the rescue again, massaged my knee and informed me that the cruciate tendons were inflamed. She fed me anti-inflammatories and emptied a sachet of Emergen-C into my bottle as I was fatiguing fast. Now we faced a three-kilometre uphill straight. I tried all the tricks in the book to take my mind off the job in hand – mantras, headphones, bead counting, you name it – and I finally made it through the arch of strung prayer flags miles behind Carol, who was waiting patiently for me despite the intense wind-chill. We were faced with Shishapangma, Phola Ganchen and Melungtse, giantesses in their wedding gowns.

Now began the deepest road descent on Earth – four and half kilometres of it. We screamed down from the ice and frost of a Tibetan Plateau morning, the red earth and white mountains contrasting with each other perfectly, to emerge in the tropical lushness of a Nepali afternoon. As we crossed the border, the quality of the road deteriorated from brand spanking new Chinese bitumen to dirt roads, landslides and Nepali mayhem. The green richness of the Bhote Kosi gorge was surreal after the austere mountains.

We reached Kathmandu on day twenty-six, riding through a convoluted matrix of villages and back streets, past monkeys and metal workshops, bakeries and brick works, temples and shrines, everywhere a noisy jam of cars and motorbikes. After much struggle and hardship, we had finally made it. We had ridden 1,158 kilometres over the Himalaya.

I had discovered I was already well versed in the discipline and commitment needed to undergo an arduous pilgrimage. Each and every one of the mountains I had been to over the years had prepared me by increments for such a journey. And I was used to the necessary pain and discomfort. Working through epilepsy and spasticity, feeling the stab of pain in my knee with every pedal rotation, and suffering the constant ache in my lumbar spine, I was in fact grounding myself, humbling myself – just as Buddhist monks or nuns or simple pilgrims cannot go on their journey of self-discovery without a deal of discomfort.

During the ceaseless hours of meditative pedalling across the plateau, I had realised something: I had found devotion also. A devotion I had discovered a long time ago. A devotion to my own 'gods': elemental forces. The wind that scours the plateau. The burning sun of high mountains. The life-giving precipitation of snow and lashing rain. The atmosphere, that gossamer sheet protecting all life on Earth. The nitrogen, oxygen, argon and carbon dioxide in just the right amounts for our unique biology. A person certainly learns the sanctity of air when travelling in the high mountains. Most of all, the wild nature, of which I was a part.

With each and every revolution of my pedals I was transforming myself. By moving *within* that landscape, I was reaffirming my life as part *of* the landscape. I was coming home to myself, as we all do in the important grounding times of our lives. I was coming home.

3

PAIN

There are heights of the soul from where even tragedy ceases to look tragic.
— Friedrich Nietzsche, *Beyond Good and Evil*

Eggshell ice. That's what climbers call the brittle skin that encases a soft inner core of snow on a mountain. It spells danger if you mistakenly venture into its fragile midst. Depending on the steepness, it can be lethal. In the mountains of Scotland it is usually formed by storms plastering snow against a frozen waterfall, followed by water spray on the snow combined with a rapid freeze–thaw cycle. This sequence forms a hollow eggshell that insulates the interior of the icefall, with ice becoming gas without going through this liquid stage. This process of sublimation turns the whole structure into something precarious and fragile, like a rotten ladder, and just as unreliable.

While climbing a frozen waterfall called *Centre Post Direct* on the Scottish Highland mountain of Creag Meagaidh (pronounced Creg Meggie), I slammed my axe into a patch of this awful stuff. Crashing through the fragile shell, I found only soft, flyaway powder behind it. I made a hole deep enough to swallow my entire arm up to the pit. No sign of any solid ice. I tried clutching the axe-head so the shaft effectively lengthened my arm by another forearm. No luck. I still couldn't find anything of substance. I tried again, this time with both arms: a kind of Transformer front crawl, inching upward using my armpits as substitute hands. My crampons were balanced on the shell, but when I attempted to lift my left boot, my right boot cracked through the ice and sank an inch with a sickening crunch. Things could fall apart here. My feet were tingling painfully as adrenaline forced my blood to my core, and I was forced to abandon any attempt at upward progress.

I had placed two ice screws, twenty-centimetre Polish aircraft-grade titanium tubes that I'd acquired from Sean Smith, who had visited on a British Mountaineering Council exchange. One was in the gully about five metres diagonally up and right from Robert and Nick, my rope-mates. The other screw, in the last of the decent ice, was now about twenty metres below me, under a bulge, and therefore out of sight. Looking down, I saw I'd dug a sort of vertical trench up the frozen cliff, swimming against the current of gravity. I also realised I couldn't go on like this, and made the tentative decision to climb down, even though down-climbing steep ice is never easy and the downfall's fragile state made the prospect all the more speculative.

Knowing you are about to fall is a curious feeling. You are still on the climb, not in pain, still thinking and working out your next move. But I knew I was going to fall. The whole process had an inevitability about it, but you can't really just throw yourself off the cliff face. So in an effort to shorten the plummet, I instinctively made three retreating moves closer to my last protection. Then, by degrees, I parted company with Creag Meagaidh: first my left boot ground down several inches of the eggshell, forcing the burden of personal preservation on to my arms, which, though in up to the pits, simply did not have enough purchase to prevent me from losing all contact with the mountain.

I screamed, more to alert my companions than out of fear, and then embarked on my voyage through space and time. Like most dedicated climbers I know, I've taken a lot of falls – it's part of the territory – and the one thing the longer plummets have in common is that they always seem to take place in a time warp. When one is engaged in the act of falling it seems an eternity, but when one stops it is an instant: a curious and not altogether unpleasant sensation.

The first thing I recall is my ice hammer slowly coming towards my face and hitting me in the eye. Later, after the Lochaber Mountain Rescue Team had me flown to Fort William hospital, X-rays showed that the hammer had fractured the frontal bone of my skull and orbit of my right eye. Looking in the mirror I discovered my fiery red haemorrhaging eyeball, like the robot from *Terminator*.

My next memory is the crampon spikes of my right boot catching the slope as I struck a less steep portion of the gully: that fractured the medial malleolus in my ankle. Then the cartwheeling began, like the chariot race in *Ben-Hur*, all fast-spinning metal spikes, down towards the burn at the base of Glen Spean.

The rope finally came tight more than fifty metres below where I'd started my whirlwind ride a few seconds before. All was silence as I crossed the finish line, with agony coming in a close second. As I lay doubled over backwards across my waist belt, I realised that the mountain had been using me as a human yoyo on the end of a very thin and stretchy 8.8-millimetre rope. An X-ray of my back showed four out of my five lumbar vertebrae had been crushed in the fall. Altogether, only six bones broken. I had got off lightly for such a huge plunge.

My fellow guide Nick Kekus came to my aid. He fixed an anchor to the sidewall of the gully and began lowering me on a rope. I struggled to breathe as my injured back magnified every tiny protuberance I scraped across, even though he performed this operation as gingerly as possible. Finally I was slumped at the base of the wintery mountain face. Nick then abseiled down and pulled the ropes. I lay on the hard, icy ground as darkness gathered, waiting for the Lochaber crew and their big yellow helicopter. I remained there, wracked in my delirium, as each breath filled my lungs and pressed my fractured spine into the frozen ground. The night was full and dark and clear, and I became lost amongst the stars of the Cygnus Arm of our very own Milky Way.

The helicopter landed. Five burly Scots clambered out and began silently moving around me, their condensing breath billowing in the light of their headlamps. There were gruff Scottish grunts and as they slid me on to the stretcher one of the silhouetted figures tutted: 'What ha' yer done to yersen this time, Paul, yer bampot?' I think I knew him but the combination of being delirious with pain and blinded by his head torch meant I couldn't respond with my customary humour.

This particular mishap was the second of three very much life-threatening accidents that I suffered in a six-year period. The first was a thirty-metre fall into the sea in Wales, when I effectively drowned, having been underwater for ten minutes. More of that later. The final serious accident was in Tasmania on the Totem Pole. All three of these calamities were completely avoidable: If only I had not taken any risks … If only I had stayed sitting safe on the couch … If only I had not chosen to lead this kind of life … But I had. I suffered much during each of those misadventures, so much so that I now consider myself to be somewhat of an expert on the subject of pain.

It probably sounds as if I'm either unlucky, or someone you would not want to tie on to a rope with. On the other hand, the list of highly proficient climbers who have fallen is a long one. It can be a fine line between clinging on successfully with your fingertips miles above your last piece of protection and making one tiny mistake that smashes you up. And when one operates on that fine line, accidents are bound to happen occasionally. That's the reality of climbing.

Some of the most proficient climbers of all time have died doing what they love: Wanda Rutkiewicz, John Bachar, Anatoli Boukreev, Alison Hargreaves. So, while I would not wish a broken back, broken limbs, several skull fractures, an acquired brain injury, hemiplegia, post-traumatic epilepsy, aphasia, dysphasia and facial agnosia on anyone, now these things have happened to me, it seems the best course of action, if, in every way, I accept them; if I learn from them what I can, and move gloriously, albeit slowly, forward. This I consider the best course of action for all of us when misfortune occurs.

Over the years I have found that this acceptance has given me the necessary resolve to face life's vicissitudes with courage and grace. I have seen through direct experience that we can learn much through our individual misfortunes. When the worst happens, it is not the end. It is a beginning.

Furthermore, I now understand that physical pain and mental anguish are but two sides of the same coin. They both have the same root cause, the same neural signatures. In a study conducted in 2013 at the University of British Columbia, people experiencing despair and existential dread took paracetamol and reported feeling better. Of course, I'm not condoning taking painkillers to avoid those things that makes us human, the wellspring of all great art and philosophy. No, it is simply to point out that physical pain is also an emotional, subjective experience.

When, because of my disabilities, I go careering off a steep mountain path and bust my face up on the rocks, and twist my arm painfully, and cut my hand, I don't only feel pain. At the same time I am disappointed in myself and momentarily angry at the situation. The crisis amplifies itself. However, as time goes by, I am learning not to be so reactive. Though pain and grief will strike everyone sooner or later, a person has to be given the space to feel what they feel. Everyone is going to come unstuck at some point in life. Everyone is going to have a worst day. It is how we *react* to that pain when it happens that makes the difference. Our relationship to pain determines how much we suffer.

I have said it before, many times: the accident on the Totem Pole was the best thing that ever happened to me. Many people find this difficult to believe. 'How can becoming a hemiplegic epileptic with speech and memory difficulties be the best thing that ever happened to you?' I am asked this all the time when I give my presentations.

I don't mean in a simple *Sliding Doors* alternative reality either: that if the rock had not landed on my head, I would not have moved to Tasmania and married my nurse and ex-partner Jane, who bore us two beautiful children, Cadi and Eli. No: much more than this.

My experience on the Totem Pole taught me to be unwavering in the face of difficulty and hardship. It taught me the importance of total acceptance of the way things are, at this moment. The more we can accept the pain, be it physical or emotional, the more we understand that it will pass. Nothing is fixed and unchanging, from the pain in our bodies or minds to our existence as a physical body, which will, sooner or later, go back to the earth. This even goes for the seemingly permanent rocks of The Mountain, which are in a continuous process of erosion. Everything comes and goes; impermanence is the natural law, the way of the universe. And everything means everything, including mental conditions such as pain and pleasure, which are nothing but constructs of the mind.

Daily pains remind me of this lesson. First thing on waking in the morning, I untie the fisherman's knot of my fingers caused by spasticity in the night and wrestle my forearm down to ninety degrees from my bicep. I often fall on the floor on my way to the bathroom; I go down like a felled tree, so these spills often result in bruising and grazing. I catch my spastic elbow painfully on the doorframe and then take a shower, which is always a dangerous operation. I laboriously get dressed, using one hand and my teeth, and teeter down the stairs. I take an anticonvulsant before I have a fit, and then munch a mouthful of dry toast, alternating this with a nibble of butter because it's too difficult to spread with the knife. Facing these hardships is as much a gift as it is a test.

My day-to-day challenges are considerably more than many people face, and considerably fewer than others. Every single one of us struggles in a multitude of ways, but I regard my relationship with struggle as precious. I consider my own pains a gift because they force me to gird my resolve and make the most of each day. Otherwise, I would never get out of bed. And this resolve includes giving thanks for the many good things in my life: the health that I have (it could be a lot worse), my wonder-filled children, my lovely partner and my wealth of friends. In this way I see suffering as a privilege that can transform daily hardships into a kind of blessing.

A most important aspect of going through our own suffering is that we in turn find it easier to relate to another being's suffering, because we have been through it ourselves. Each time we feel pain, it acts as a reminder, bringing us back down to earth. Our own personal pain can increase our ability to feel compassion; and undergoing hardship, if we are mindful about what that hardship entails, can lead us to empathise more freely.

On a personal level, before my accident I was a very driven and self-motivated climber. Family birthdays, the partner in my life and other important events always came second to The Mountain. My mother wouldn't see me for five or six months at a time while I climbed. More than one girlfriend became bored of waiting for me to return from some far-flung expedition. Of course, I was in my early twenties, the age when we more easily feel the tight grip of obsession.

After my three climbing accidents, I began noticing other individuals' various hardships and needs. I was becoming incrementally more empathetic. I must add to this: one of the benefits of having children is that it instils the quality of empathy in the parent. You can't often come first when you are looking after a child. On top of that, the selfish climber no longer existed even if, paradoxically, I needed all the qualities that falling rock had instilled in me.

Most of the time, we view life through a lens distorted by our desires, our regrets, our expectations. Pain brings us deafeningly into the present. We cannot avoid being here, now, to borrow a phrase from that master of psychedelia, Ram Dass. Everything about discomfort can provide a window for us to see things as they really are. I realise that the experience of pain is different for each of us. Yet I've come to believe we can accept pain and remain composed. I also realise that for some this may require Buddha-like levels of equanimity.

If we can achieve this, we can do nothing other than be transported into another realm. A plane beyond enduring.

There are ways to train the mind to come to a greater acceptance of pain. Even though I have fallen long distances in the mountains, smashed myself up and endured inordinate amounts of physical pain, it was not until I began to practise Vipassana meditation that I realised how little I knew. One isn't supposed to endure pain with a kind of Victorian stiff upper lip. (I'm reminded here of Lord Paget, said to have uttered the immortal phrase, 'By God, sir, I seem to have lost my leg,' at the battle of Waterloo. The story is apocryphal, but his stoicism was real. His pulse barely altered as the surgeon removed the injured leg without anaesthetic.) No, if we accept pain and practise non-reaction, we learn to be a witness to our pain and see it for what it really is – an ephemeral sensation. It's what our mind does with pain that ushers in suffering.

I was intrigued by pain. I wanted to know what pain was. Where did it come from? How could I lessen it without depending on drugs? I wanted to explore, and perhaps find a remedy for, the pain I often feel in my neck and shoulders caused by the injury, plus the constant ache in my elbow and leg produced by the spastic hemiplegia. Oh, and I shouldn't forget the agony I often endure in my lumbar spine from that Meagaidh screamer. I had long taken a cocktail of the opiate Endone, marketed in the United States as OxyContin, and ibuprofen to manage the more extreme pain events. Was it possible to control pain without drugs? I had heard incredible, let us say improbable, things about Vipassana. That it can permanently cure mental and emotional problems as well as physical pain. That it was mind over matter. I had to leave my scepticism behind and give it a try. For this ten-day experiment I would leave my painkillers at home, and – this may have been a mistake – my anticonvulsant medications too.

Ten years or so after the Totem Pole accident, I went on a Vipassana meditation course. After driving halfway up a mountain, my partner, Melinda, dropped me at a collection of huts deep in a forest in southern Tasmania. There, I met twenty-four strangers and sat down on the floor with them for 110 silent hours. Sceptical, but willing to give anything a go, I was to delve more deeply into the nature of pain than I had ever done on the mountain.

The very word *Vipassana* might sound like mystical nonsense, but it's simply the Pali word for 'insight', Pali being the Indo-European language spoken by the Buddha. It is the form of meditation Gautama taught in north-eastern India for forty-five years, one of scores of forms of meditation. There is no communication for ten days: no speaking, no eye contact, no messages. There are no pens or paper allowed, no books and definitely no phones or tablets. No distractions whatsoever. You are imprisoned in the grounds and men and women are segregated. You spend the ten days inside your own head. You eat little and essentially live a monastic life.

Vipassana is powerful stuff. One woman blew out her eardrum on day seven and blood started to trickle down her earlobe. The same day, a man had a full-on breakdown and left the course in tears. A day later, another student had some sort of fit. I was sitting behind him and couldn't help opening my eyes just a tiny crack. I saw that he was convulsing rhythmically in waves. Then he began violently shaking. All this came about just sitting there in a room. To a casual observer, we were doing nothing.

I had a headache for the first three days and began hearing peals of bells on day three, as my headache subsided. What sounded like wedding bells lasted until day nine. Afterwards, a friend told me this was very auspicious; several of the great meditators, including Gurdjieff, had heard bells. I wasn't sure I believed him. On the other hand, all the significant events of the day – 4 a.m. wake-up, 4.30 call to begin sitting, 6.30 breakfast, etc. – were all marked by bells, and I often mistook these for the bells inside my head. Consequently, I missed several mealtimes. However, Gol, one of the volunteer servers, always came looking for me. You are watched carefully for any kind of mental breakdown, especially if you are a new student. This going down so deeply into your own head can be dangerous.

On day seven I had my first seizure in four years. I was in my cell
taking time out from the main group to meditate alone when I began
to experience the familiar taste of iron in my mouth. I thought, 'Here
we go.' I knew this aura well. I began to drool and the whole right side
of my face dropped (I always picture Charles Laughton playing
Quasimodo in the 1939 version of *The Hunchback of Notre Dame* when-
ever I have a seizure). My tongue felt foreign and huge, like a shoe in
my mouth, and the right side of my body convulsed with agonising
pins and needles. After a fit, I have to sleep for the rest of the day,
so I made my excuses to Gol.

I kept the distressing news of the seizure to myself because I didn't
want to get thrown off the course. I already knew I was experiencing
one of the most profound events of my life. Yet, this frightening situation was also accompanied by some truly marvellous happenings.
Firstly, I noticed the forest wallabies were communicating with me –
not talking, you understand, but whispering with their eyes, calming
me, telling me not to worry. Thank God everyone had made a vow of
silence so I couldn't share my Doctor Dolittle experience. Crazier
still, during one prolonged sit, I fully extended three fingers of my
right hand for the first time in seventeen years.

The process of Vipassana is complicated, but put simply it works
like this: you are asked to direct your entire attention towards a single
point on the body – the shoulder, for instance – and passively observe
it until you notice a feeling, any feeling: an itch, a pain, a tingling. The
particular feelings are different for everyone, but I seemed to be
particularly receptive. Before long, whatever part of my body I pointed
my attention to became a mass of sensation. We were told by S.N.
Goenka, the Burmese businessman turned global Vipassana teacher,
via video-link and from beyond the grave, that this was due to the
nature of all matter, from rocks and metals to flesh and blood; that all
matter is made of vibrating particles, dying and being reborn. (Goenka
was a veritable rock star to his tens of thousands of followers, although
I imagine having to remain sober and composed meant he couldn't

really revel in his status.) By getting in tune with our bodies we become aware of this mass of electromagnetic activity. These sub-atomic particles Gautama called *kalapas*, something he observed by direct experience by practising Vipassana meditation two and a half millennia ago. Once you approach your ninetieth hour of sitting there cross-legged with eyes closed, you begin to realise, not on an intellectual level but on an experiential level, that all matter is made of the same stuff.

During one intense *adhitthana* (sitting of strong determination), with all the students sitting as still as a statue for an hour, I found myself enduring great pain in my back from the break I suffered on Meagaidh. Thirty minutes I could take. By forty minutes, things were beginning to unravel. By fifty I was in agony. A war started raging within me. We had been warned about this: how if we react to these pains and become pissed off, it will eventually give rise to hating situations and to hating others. In the real world it is not much of a step from being reactive to seething with jealousy and bad-mouthing others. The next thing you know you're marching down the street wearing the wrong kind of swastika. But it was in the last ten minutes that I did my best work.

My body dissolved into millions of blue and yellow subatomic particles. It then exploded and all these tiny particles went flying around, like in a dandelion-seed storm. Later that day, when I told my teacher about my experience, during a special one-on-one conference, permitted to discuss problems with the regimen, he said I was mistaken to gain pleasure from my experience. I needed to further practise non-reaction. While I was in the midst of the trip, I began to suspect that someone with an ulterior motive had assembled us here, in this Tasmanian forest, and dropped acid in the water tank.

There is a story popular in Llanberis, the mountain village in North Wales where I used to live. It concerns Cliff Phillips, a legendary climber from the 1970s. It is said he slipped LSD in the reservoir above the village and all the townsfolk turned into drop-leaf tables and fish.

The writer and climber Jim Perrin, who is no stranger himself to psychedelics, interviewed author and ordained Buddhist monk Peter Matthiessen, collected in the essays *Yes, To Dance*. Matthiessen, talking about the mystical effects of LSD, said that through meditation he could arrive at the same place, without the chemical mist.

We have all heard, if not experienced, how pain can transport us, offer us a glimpse of another realm. It's true. We can. If we allow ourselves to, we can unshackle ourselves from the burden of rationality. We can peer through the crack in the middle of the 'doors of perception'.

The pain one forces oneself to endure while sitting in meditation can be likened to the hardships and deprivations endured on The Mountain. Mountaineering history books are full of climbers under great stress at high altitude being aware of the presence of a 'third man' travelling near them, looking out for them. There are plenty of instances recorded on the upper slopes of Everest. British mountaineer Doug Scott had lengthy conversations with his feet as he endured his night out on Everest's south summit (Scott described it as third and fourth man syndrome – the third man being his left foot and the fourth man the right).

These examples could be put down to the hallucinations of a hypoxic brain. I would argue that they had reached a heightened state of awareness: the state Abraham Maslow calls the peak-experience. Usually associated with art and religion, or experiences in the natural world, 'the peak-experience,' Maslow said, 'points to a place of effortlessness, without fear, self-doubt or self-criticism, without time or space, a place of transcendence'. Peak-experience is usually associated with a state of flow, but I would argue that it can also be accessed through the door of great hardship. Maslow's ideas fell out of fashion, partly due to a lack of empirical support, but he wrote with real insight into the human condition. Personally, I think Maslow was on to something.

It was during Vipassana meditation that I learnt we can reach just such a sublime place, a place where suffering does not exist, through deprivation, discomfort and pain. During that *adhitthana*, I realised I wasn't suffering any longer; my pain had disintegrated along with my body. This was the profound moment that I realised that by being non-reactive I could simply observe my pain compassionately, as though it were not my pain but someone else's. A good feeling, a bad feeling, it didn't make any difference. They were both impermanent manifestations of subatomic vibrations.

There is another important element to this: physical pain and emotional pain are processed in very similar ways in the brain. As Gautama Buddha said, all pain 'is mind-wrought'. This means that if we do not react to negative events, like getting punched or bereaved, we can see them clearly and objectively as impermanent. I'm not saying grieving is bad or wrong. Far from it. It is very beneficial to go through the grieving process, but if we want to come out the other end, and resist the temptation to let it take over our lives, we must not become attached to our grief. We must simply observe it and let it go when we are ready.

The whole process of a ten-day Vipassana course is akin to climbing a big wall. On a big climb, there are long periods of intense concentration, where one taps home a piton or fiddles in a marginal stopper. A whole day can pass on a long artificial pitch just for a climber to achieve a rope-length. That may be eight hours of intense concentration, so to draw parallels with *adhitthana* would not be a rash comparison. Added to this are the psychological stresses and ever-present dangers of any ascent. There are stark similarities between the discomforts of *adhitthana* and the extreme discomforts climbers are forced to endure on The Mountain: freezing cold bivouacs, swollen, frost-nipped hands, hanging in a harness all day with an empty stomach. Just as it is not abnormal to spend the odd three days without food on an alpine ascent, so 'old students' (those who have endured a Vipassana course before) must fast for eighteen hours a day.

Even route-finding on a big wall has similarities to Vipassana: if you are climbing a new route, you are really making it up as you go along; you don't know what that cliff is going to drop on you next. In a similar way, with Vipassana one never knows what horrors from the blackest corners of one's psyche are going to rise to the surface. The whole process leads to an intense confrontation with oneself. Some do not like what they see. Whether hanging in a harness or sitting cross-legged on the floor, both the climber and the meditator gain access to a wealth of self-knowledge.

During the long hours of sitting, the mind inevitably wanders. Besides the usual sexual fantasies, I had a sterling idea for a hom-unculus doll for children. Like the Stretch Armstrong doll I had as a kid, children would be able to stretch his arms, legs and other appendages to great lengths. There were lots of amputation hallu-cinations, including taking off my useless right arm and having it stuffed by a taxidermist and mounted in a crimp position so that I could take it to the crag and hang it on a finger edge. There was the elaborate self-operated cigar guillotine for my little finger. It's always getting in the way, that pinkie. I plotted to chop off the useless digit, film the process and upload it to YouTube. Maybe it would go viral.

By the ninth day, we were studying sensations within our bodies and 'sweeping en masse' (scanning the whole body). Each person feels something different. I was experiencing a tingling, like pins and needles, the whole length of me, inside and outside. The tingling began on the crown of my head and ended at the tip of my toes, like a bucket of hot water being poured over me, and then back up as if I was being submerged in a hot pool. These sensations were much more pronounced on my healthy left side. Having hemiplegia means reduced blood flow, cold extremities and reduced feeling all down one side of the body, in my case the right side. So, I had to work at detecting the tingling down that half.

The sensation I was now experiencing throughout my body bore more than a passing similarity to the seizures I had endured for the past eighteen years. (Fifteen years earlier, I was having up to ten seizures a day.) I took a mind-altering concoction of anticonvulsants back then, but now I was starting to suspect that the seizures were the body's way of attempting to repair itself, and that seizure medication was hindering my recovery. I knew this to be a risky hypothesis and so decided to treat it with equanimity: 'It is what it is,' a great sage (read stoner) from Llanberis used to say. Neither good nor bad.

On a subsequent ten-day course, I had what I like to call my Joan of Arc moment. I was deep in meditation, sweeping en masse, when Goenka asked us to drive our attention through our bodies, stabbing this way and that. It wasn't painful, even though it does feel like you are being skewered. I then took it upon myself to begin feeling my individual organs. First my liver, then each of my kidneys. Reaching my left lung, I ran the back of my attention up the frills of my alveoli. But it was when I cradled my heart in my awareness that things started to go weird. I began to have a seizure and let out an audible sob. Opening my eyes, I found myself to be blind: just a mass of colourful patterns before my eyes. I sprang up and staggered about my cell, leaning against the walls. For the first time I had quelled a fit, leading me to think I could bring one on as and when I pleased. My heart rate returned to normal, and at length my vision returned.

Whatever tiny area I directed my attention to now felt as though it were being prodded with a hot poker, but the sensation was intensely agreeable. Then I recalled Goenka telling us from the screen that one should never place a value judgement on any feeling, pleasant or unpleasant, as this risks all one's hard work coming to nothing. Judgement is reaction and in this place one is taught not to react, not to scratch that itch, not to brush away that fly that has landed on the end of your nose: just observe. Just observe. One must remain balanced and composed in Vipassana, as in life. And in the same way, one will not survive long on The Mountain without a certain level-headedness.

On day ten, we were allowed to speak. It would be too much of a culture shock, and potentially dangerous, to be released back into the bustle of the city without the buffer of a day. Everyone had big grins pasted to their faces. Someone asked me, 'How did you go?' I was excited, and having been silent for nine days wanted to tell him everything I had learnt all at once, yet when I opened my mouth, all that came out was a tiny squeak. I had lost my voice and wouldn't regain it fully for days. I felt humbled, driving away. All the cooks, helpers and teachers are volunteers, and at the end of ten days, if you found that you got no benefit from the practice, you are asked not to pay *dana*.[1]

In terms of mental anguish, my experiment with Vipassana was like climbing El Capitan. The pain and fear I experienced made for some of the hardest and most rewarding days of my life. During those ten days I learnt how to accept and be equanimous with discomfort. I discovered that once I gave up fighting and simply accepted the pain, all conflict ceased.

I remember watching *Lawrence of Arabia* with my father for the umpteenth time; he loved the film, having served in Aqaba just after the Second World War. Early in the film, Peter O'Toole lights a cigarette and extinguishes the match between his thumb and fore-finger. William Potter, a humble corporal, furtively attempts the same and burns his fingers:

'Ooh! It damn well 'urts!'
'Certainly it hurts.'
'What's the trick, then?'
'The trick, William Potter, is not minding that it hurts.'

By not reacting, we find strength inside us and can move beyond not just pain, but suffering also.

Learning how to cope with epilepsy was different. My fits are not only painful but also disorienting and confusing. It is difficult in the extreme to remain equanimous when your brain is confused and you

---

1   *Dana*: Pali for 'donation'.

don't even know your own name. During an episode, I remember just fragments and, sitting here writing this, I have the impression of my mind becoming a blank slate. I used to get very distressed by losing my memory for what feels like hours. Now I see I have a choice to either hate it or accept it, to attempt to derive some meaning from my epilepsy. By adopting this attitude, I have stumbled upon a font of personal compassion, grace and strength. Each time I have a fit, the pain is intense, as if my hand and foot are being immersed in boiling water. I drool. I am transported (even though I must declare the fact of my seizure to the authorities and accept a driving ban). I transcend. With each seizure I find a little more strength and determination to continue.

* * *

DECEMBER 2015, HIGH SUMMER

I was about to tackle lutruwita's (Tasmania's) Point to Pinnacle, a race the media had dubbed 'The World's Toughest Half Marathon'. The course stretches twenty-one kilometres from sea level near the city of nipaluna (Hobart), to the summit of kunanyi (Mount Welling-ton) at 1,271 metres. I was aiming to be the first 'adaptive cycle' entrant. The local newspaper dubbed me a 'wheelchair athlete', but there are two problems with this moniker: I don't use a wheelchair (it is a recumbent trike) and I'm more an advanced potterer than an athlete. They also included a Superman logo in the corner of my story, which I did not complain about.

My plan was all worked out, right down to the therapeutic botu-linum toxin shots I had five days before the race: eleven injections in my right arm; seven in the right leg; eight in the right side of my back. These were to combat my ever-increasing spasticity. I was feeling nice and loose and training every day for kunanyi's steep hairpin ascent.

Then, three days before the race, my well-organised world began to crumble. I felt myself being shaken from a deep sleep by a woman I didn't recognise. The light above the bed seemed intolerably bright and my tongue (or at least, the lump of meat inside my mouth, for at this moment I can hardly name anything) felt twice its normal size.

'Paul! What's wrong?'

'Wha … ?' Apparently, I had been clawing at her back. And the right side of my face was all droopy.

'What's my name?'

At that moment she didn't even look familiar.

'Who the hell are you?' I wanted to shout.

I couldn't answer. I didn't know Melinda's name even though we'd been sleeping in the same bed for the past five years.

'Can you tell me the kids' names?'

I could not. Although I was dimly aware that I had kids, I couldn't think how many.

'Okay, can you tell me the time?'

I wanted to scream, 'Never mind the time! Where the hell are we?'

At last, though, Melinda's face was beginning to seem more familiar, so I attempted to comply. I tried to read the digital display on the bedside table, but the numbers wouldn't align. 'Twenty … sixty,' I guessed, but couldn't verbalise it anyway. It was 12.20 a.m.

Melinda was worried as I was struggling to breathe. My airway was being constricted.

'I'm going to call for an ambulance.'

I attempted to dissuade her, which involved me mumbling something and tugging on her shirt. The one thing I could clearly see was the sequence of events about to unfold: the driving ban, the blood tests, followed by having to go back on fatiguing anticonvulsants. I was taking a break from them and the foggy mind they gave me.

Slowly, things were coming back to me. I now knew my partner's name began with the letter 'M'. The woman whose name began with 'M' dialled triple zero and twenty minutes later I was being bundled into an ambulance. A flashing warning light was pointing to the letters S T R O K E, so they took me to the emergency department of the

Royal Hobart Hospital, a place I knew well. Here I spent the night on a stretcher with a thin blanket pulled over my head in an attempt to block out the fluorescent lighting. It turned out I had experienced a rather sizeable seizure, my first for a while.

The next three days leading up to the race were spent in bed ruminating on the frailty of human existence. I knew I'd been closer to dying on Creag Meagaidh, the Totem Pole, and the day I fell off a cliff into the Irish Sea (as I said, more about that later, in the Chapter 'Death'). Oh, and when I stepped out into traffic in Barcelona. I also knew that on each of these occasions, the feeling, the learning, the *benefit* I gained from these experiences – acceptance, courage, and even a grace of sorts – seemed to fade away. Nonetheless, with each plummet into misery I was learning how to harness these benefits that much more, and was now at least attempting to live each day with more presence, as if it were my last. I truly believe that if we let ourselves recall those times when we have been made aware of our own mortality, when we are a whisker from death or in severe pain, we will find it easier to live right now, in this moment. After all, this moment is all we have.

The day before the race, still feeling dizzy and fatigued, I called my doctor. He thought it was madness to continue and warned me not to go near kunanyi. However, I figured if I did start to feel pre-ictal – I normally feel a welling up of emotion, followed by an aroma in my dead olfactory cortex and a metallic taste in my mouth – I could just turn around and free-wheel back down the hill. I have learnt so much from my suffering that each fall or even stubbed toe seems loaded with meaning.

The Catholic priest and writer Richard Rohr talks about 'necessary suffering' and how if you try to avoid suffering in your life you end up suffering ten times more. Although the Buddha's near contemporary Aeschylus put it more adroitly in the chorus of *Agamemnon*:

He who learns must suffer.
And even in our sleep, pain, which cannot forget,
falls drop by drop upon the heart,
until, in our own despair, against our will,
comes wisdom through the awful grace of God.

I feel a bond with Aeschylus because he died from a head injury, struck by a tortoise dropped from the heavens by a bearded vulture. I am comforted by the thought that he did not suffer, since there are no pain receptors in the brain.

So, with the support of Melinda, I made the somewhat burdensome decision to start the race anyway. On the morning, we arose at five, having prepared brown rice and lentil congee in the slow cooker overnight for a 'power breakfast'. I had abstained from coffee for a few days previously and my espresso was giving me a buzz.

Three thousand entrants were gathered at the start line. I was feeling rather dizzy, but put that down to our early start. I focused on summoning my determination, as though I were hand-picking posies of monkshood and saxifrage on The Mountain. As the only person on wheels, sitting down, I had to be careful not to ram the sprocket on my pedal cranks into the calves of the runners around me. Travelling low to the ground like this, my eyeline was level with throngs of lycra-clad backsides, and I had a wide grin pasted to my face.

As the first person on wheels to attempt the race up kunanyi, the organisers had requested someone accompany me to make sure I didn't veer off the road and go over a cliff. Melinda readily agreed. She often provided the perfect foil to my, at times, overzealous commitment to completing a course, any course. She checked in on me at regular intervals, even though she was finding it no pushover herself. And while some might describe me as recklessly determined, I had no desire to invite a seizure, and so paced myself in the initial stages.

The route was lined with bizarre demonstrations of support. There were front rooms erected on the roadside complete with settees and standard lamps; there were kilt-wearing bagpipers and young High-land flingers; there was a pop-up cafe supplying coffee halfway and, at the fourteen-kilometre mark, a DJ spinning trance. Then I strained on the pedals as I turned up the Pinnacle Road for the climb proper.

Above the car park at The Springs, the forest became less massive and the vegetation changed from great gums to telopea, banksia and hakia, the remnants of the supercontinent of Gondwana. The angle of the terrain also changed, steepening by five degrees between kilometres fourteen and eighteen. This stretch of road is the crux of the whole Point to Pinnacle and marked a period of deep digging for me. With each revolution I was gasping for air. Even though my thighs were burning as I pushed with everything I had on the pedals, the other competitors were still pulling gradually away from me. I didn't care. I just wanted to make it to the top of the mountain without having a fit, and inside the cut-off time of four hours and forty minutes.

Rounding the Big Bend, three kilometres from the top and at over 1,000 metres in altitude, I knew from past experience that I would likely be facing a ferociously cold headwind. This concerned, even frightened, me. But the gods were smiling on me. On this most perfect of days, as the low forest gave way to alpine scenery, there wasn't even a breeze.

Tim Smith, the race organiser, ran beside me for the final 300 metres. I had three minutes before the cut-off time and automatic disqualification, so Tim counted down to the moment it would be all over for me. Luckily, I had just gobbled the last of my energy gels and was feeling a surge of life.

'Two minutes.'

Legs pumping, I still had a rope-length to go.

'One minute thirty seconds.'

Keep pedalling.

'One ten.'

I could ignore the burning in my legs, but my lungs felt like they were going to explode.

'One minute.'

Not far now.

'Fifty seconds ...'

Yards.

'Forty.'

I made it over the finish line with just thirty-seven seconds to spare.

The mountain erupted in a great cheer, even though the race winner had crossed the line three hours before me. All my teammates had waited on the finish line. And as I seemed to be having some problems walking, we decided to take the waiting bus back down the mountain.

4

FEAR

... That which is
Can never cease to be; that which is not
Will not exist. To see this truth of both
Is theirs who part essence from accident,
Substance from shadow. Indestructible,
Learn thou! the Life is, spreading life through all;
It cannot anywhere, by any means,
Be anywise diminished, stayed, or changed.
But for these fleeting frames which it informs
With spirit deathless, endless, infinite,
They perish. Let them perish, Prince! And fight!

— *Bhagavad Gita*, Chapter 2, verses 51—61

Mario was driving at speed down the narrow streets of Arco. I was clutching on to the 'chicken handle' with my good left arm across my body as he left town and raced through fragrant olive groves. As Lake Garda came into the rear-view mirror, we hit the gravel of the car park and skidded to an abrupt stop.

On the path up to the Placche di Baone I paused to recover my equanimity and found myself gazing with astonishment at the neon green of moss on a limestone boulder. Tiny droplets of dew clung to

delicate sporophytes. Each dewdrop had a dazzling microscopic pin-
point of light: whole spiral galaxies on one simple clump of moss.
However, just as I was becoming fixated on this 'universe in a grain of
sand', a giant woodlouse bulldozed its way through, destroying entire
solar systems.

At the bottom of the crag, sitting on a fallen tree, I silently prepared
my climbing rack. It was far from a difficult climb; the higher reaches
seemed to blend into the hillside as odd grassy tufts gave way to a full,
green-carpeted embankment. I have friends who would have relished
climbing this cliff in a 'no-hands' style to pep up the challenge. Still,
this was *my* moment, not theirs. I was about to embark on my first
post-accident lead climb. I would be going first, making the clips.
Climbers like to call it 'the sharp end'. It was more than a decade since
my Totem Pole calamity but it felt far less.

I heard foreign voices; a colourful group of Czechs were preparing
to climb the slab also. They were dressed as if they had escaped from
the Eurovision Song Contest, all hair and happy pants. I squinted up
at the sky. A solitary bird of prey was circling high above.

Climbing partners mentally sign a contract of great importance. It
is a contract that should not be entered into lightly. Mario and I had
been great friends ever since I ended his climbing career by acciden-
tally dropping a block sixty metres on to him, shattering his tibia and
fibula. We hadn't climbed together since then. As we were on a remote
mountain in Patagonia at the time, Mario endured a three-day rescue,
being dragged down a glacier in a rolled-up tent fly back to base camp.
During this morphine-soaked descent, a hideous infection crept in
and he almost lost his foot. There could be no other choice but Mario
for such an auspicious climb.

Placche di Baone's unique cliff caters specifically for para-climbers
(climbers with disabilities), and is the first 'no frontiers' climbing wall
in the world. The climbs are wheelchair accessible with the names and
grades written in Braille at the base. Some routes have a bolt every
metre, preventing a climber falling far. By contrast, my chosen route,

Bottoni Bianco (White Buttons), had eight-metre run-outs between the bolts: just four spaced bolts in total for the whole climb.

This meant that if I was to slip when clipping one bolt I would fall – or rather slide, roll and bounce – eight metres to the previous bolt, then eight metres past that bolt for a grand total of sixteen metres, though once you add the rope stretch (modern ropes are like elastic bands in comparison to old-school ropes) and account for slack in the system, I would have fallen at least twenty metres: sixty-five feet in old money. Not only is that a hell of a long way to fall, but the angle of the slab and the rough rock meant I would be grated, like a cheese, all the way down. Falling was not something I could contemplate, but contemplate I must as it was a distinct possibility.

There is an old climbers' adage that states 'THE LEADER MUST NOT FALL'. This goes all the way back to when a climber used to tie a brittle hemp rope around the waist and set off up a cliff with just a few looped rope slings for protection. If a climber fell in those days, he (in the Victorian era 'the sharp end' was almost invariably reserved for the man, as it was considered no place for 'the gentler sex') would smash himself up, have severe internal injuries from the rope and likely die. Climbing began to get much safer with the advent of dynamic ropes and modern hardware such as metal wedges or nuts, and then camming devices. However, the old adage still rang true in the 1980s with climbs such as *The Indian Face* on Clogwyn Du'r Arddu and *The Bells! The Bells!* at Gogarth, both crags in North Wales. On these climbs, and a whole host of others first done in that era, the lack of protection was such, and the danger so great, that just like in the nineteenth century, if you fell you would likely die. So here was I now, repeating that old adage like a mantra: 'I must not fall. I must not fall'.

Standing at the foot of the giant low-angled slab, tying on to the rope with one hand, I had to pay special attention to get it right. It was a figure-of-eight knot; you thread the rope through a figure-of-eight shape you've already tied before you push the end through your harness. It's one of those knots that if you get it wrong it's still likely to work. Then I squeaked the smooth black rubber soles of my climbing shoes. I was now trembling with fear. That didn't seem at all strange to me. Everyone gets scared, just as all animals experience fear; it's the 'flight' in the 'fight or flight' response. Pancho, our family's rescued greyhound, cowers when strangers come to pat him from above instead of showing him their palm from below. That will be conditioning from his previous owner, a racing kennel. Wild animals live in a 'landscape of fear', surrounded by threats they must avoid in order to have a chance at reproduction. There is no way of avoiding fear. Fear is reality. It is not something that must be overcome. One must befriend fear, really cosy up to it. To use a later cliché, everyone must at some point 'do it scared'.

As a teenager, I had a copy of *Mountaineering: The Freedom of the Hills* on virtually permanent loan from Bolton Library. This was the second edition, published in the year of my birth, 1967. It warned how 'the climber must maintain three points of contact with the rock at all times'. This is tricky for a hemiplegic. As only my left side functions properly, I really only have two points of contact plus a very shaky third point, my right foot, with its paralysed and floppy ankle. Thus, with a maximum potential three points of contact, I can only maintain two points of contact if I'm going to move one of them up. And two points of contact, like walking a tightrope, is inherently unstable. Even on a low-angled slab my climbing style was a series of dynamic hand slaps and foot hops.

Like a drunk trying to get home from the pub, I staggered up the lower section of the cliff. My heart was throbbing and I was so scared my right side stiffened with spasticity. And yet, approaching the first bolt, I felt like the drunk was indeed finding his way back home. One metre above the bolt and I was fumbling with the key in the lock. I already felt vulnerable. But it was when I ventured to two metres that I fell through the door and the real fun began. I found myself teetering further and deeper into the darkness. There was, however, a residue of the old boldness I used to possess, and I could not stop myself from moving ever upward, making moves I could not reverse, going deeper into the unknown. There was another old adage that I sometimes climbed by: 'Never climb up what you can't reverse.' I relied on it while soloing, but when I was tied into a rope, I would show a deliberate disregard for this 'old-fashioned' rule.

At three metres out from my last protection bolt, I was facing a fall of maybe eight metres, factoring in rope stretch. That's more than a standard two-storey house, a hell of a long way for someone who can't control the way they fall and is bound to plummet like a sack of spuds.

At four metres, my body became a black cavern, a grotto, my ribs stalactites. There was a heart, my heart, attached by wires to the stalactites. Its beat was deafening: thud-THUD, thud-THUD. This beating of my heart seemed to be causing the cliff to quake … wait … yes it was really shaking! Later, Davide, who was hanging above me taking photographs, said he could hear my heart beating from several metres away.

Five metres out could have been five miles as far as my body was concerned. The quaking of the cliff was causing the whole face to fracture. Hairline fissures were spreading down the slab toward me … first vertically downward with an audible 'craaack' … then right-angling … then carrying on their jagged descent until the tiny fissures passed directly between my legs.

My mind was pleading for help, but at the same time my body climbed on. 'One more move wouldn't hurt.' It was as if there were three of us on that climb that day: my fearful mind, my brutish body, overriding the mind and its attempts to say no, and someone or something else. There was another entity, neither mind nor body, somewhere outside, beyond both, looking on. Was it keeping the other two safe? It had better.

At six metres, and only at six metres, I began to surface. Bubbles like crystal globes floated up, filtering the light, and it was tempting to rise with them at the same velocity, but I had to avoid rushing … Slow down … I was now up against a seventeen-metre fall if I muffed it.

White light, blinding me … Fresh air, lots of it, I found I could breathe, like a diver surfacing … There was the cold breath of a breeze on my sweat-streaked cheek. I peered down between my legs where the rope hung prophylactically. I could see Mario poised to sprint off and take in all that rope should I fall. I could hear the chatter of the Czechs on the ground (what were they talking about?).

Seven metres. My friend the third entity hovered above my mind and body for what seemed like an aeon. This consciousness was attached to my physical body by a string on an inertia reel, like the keys on a security guard's waist or a dog on one of those extendable leads. Suddenly, the inertia reel retracted, and my friend came crashing back into my body, which was mid-tripod move. Placche di Baone became a white room, at once both expansive, like a vast echoey cathedral, and tight, like a brightly painted but claustrophobic cupboard.

Eight metres. My body and my consciousness expanded to include the whole world. In that moment I was a little child in a Bolton council house … A great forest … I was ocean-sized … I was a mountain and a mosquito simultaneously … I was at once as powerful as a volcano and more vulnerable than a daisy in a meadow … Perfect. I pulled the rope up and, with a metallic 'clip', as satisfying as any sound in the world, I was safe.

I knew right away that this was one of those rare moments of which one has only perhaps a handful in one's life. Something always to be striven for but not often attainable. When all around me, the cliff, the sky, the trees below, turned white, I knew I was having another visit from old friend Abraham Maslow and his peak-experience. It felt like his description of 'limitless horizons opening up to the vision, the feeling of being simultaneously more powerful and also more helpless than one ever was before, the feeling of great ecstasy and wonder and awe, the loss of placing in time and space'.

A feeling that something infinitely profound and valuable had just taken place. Something transformative.

After taking a handful of moments to normalise my pulse and breathing, I gazed out over the terracotta roofs of Arco, towards Lake Garda. I sighed a contented sigh. Then I descended and gave Mario a brotherly hug. I remarked to my belayer that I thought the climb dangerously under-graded at 2c and considered it was worthy of at least 3b, both absurdly easy grades for me in my past life. We also talked of the paradox of easier climbs: how they invariably tend to be more dangerous than their harder counterparts, being generally of low angle and unprotected. Chatter really that, for me, concealed the gravitas of what had just occurred.

For years I have been playing out that day, that climb on Placche di Baone. Something had piqued my imagination. Beginning with that one climb, I have had a growing fascination with lead rock climbing as a path to self-fulfilment, self-realisation. I know it has been written about in countless books, journals and magazines, that rock climbing has beneficial effects on one's health. But it always sounded trite to me: statements like 'Climbing puts the mundanity of daily life into perspective.' ... 'The challenge of climbing fosters self-reliance.' ... 'Climbing encourages self-discipline.' ... 'Climbing makes us more courageous.' ... 'Climbing helps us to be humbler in the face of a giant mountain.' ... 'The bond of the rope nurtures compassion.' ... and finally something about 'the spirit of adventure'. Sure, rock climbing and mountaineering can bring about all these changes in us (though I'm not quite sure what 'a spirit of adventure' entails), and it certainly has in me. I have expounded on some of those subjects in this book. But the truth is that by brushing up against death as frequently as mountaineers and climbers inevitably do, climbing must have more far-reaching consequences. The act of doing such a potentially dangerous activity, and doing it well, must bring about a profound change in an individual's psyche.

The vast majority of us go about life from day to day acting as though we are immortal. We can all intellectualise the fact that we are going to die one day, sooner or later. Most of us have said 'we may as well do it today, because tomorrow we might get hit by a bus'. But few of us really believe it. We can't seem to instinctualise it (I know 'instinctualise' isn't in the dictionary yet, but it ought to be), to process it emotionally. We're happy to fool ourselves.

This disconnect between the intellectual and the instinctual, that we know death is coming but have to find a way to function anyway, has its own area of study: Terror Management Theory (TMT). Derived from Ernest Becker's Pulitzer Prize-winning philosophical work *The Denial of Death*, the theory postulates that much human behaviour springs from our knowledge of absolute annihilation and the terror that creates. This knowledge, also known as 'mortality salience', has been on our minds ever since we developed prefrontal lobes and became Homo sapiens. It lies behind our creation of religion and our brittle self-esteem. Mortality salience suggests that all human action is directed at avoiding the shadow of death or distracting ourselves from the very idea of our extinction. 'And so,' as Becker wrote, 'we can understand what seems like an impossible paradox: the ever-present fear of death ... as well as our utter obliviousness to this fear in our conscious life.'

The Greeks enshrined this contradiction of the human heart in myth two and a half thousand years ago with the legend of Prometheus (which means 'forethought'). As punishment for stealing fire, the Titan Prometheus was chained to a mountain in the Caucasus where a giant bird swooped down daily to devour his regenerating liver. In another legend, he had warned his brother Epimetheus (meaning 'hindsight') not to marry Pandora, secretly sent by Zeus to punish humankind. And it was a bespectacled Austrian psychologist named Otto Rank who coined the term Prometheus Complex to explain how people are the only creatures on Earth aware of their own impending doom. (Although you do wonder about some other animals.) To travel beyond this terror is the only way Prometheus will be free from his chains, or we, as people, will be free from ours.

This theory, that humans want to sidestep the truth of their inevitable demise, suggests that so much of what we desire, upgrading the car or television, clamouring for a promotion at work, even going on holiday, is displacement activity rooted in the fear of death. We have to amass as much as possible, as much wealth and as many experiences as possible, before we die. We have entered a race, but there is all this stuff littering the track: new houses, foreign trips, cash everywhere, blowing around the stadium, automobiles and changes of career. The aim, it seems, is to pick it all up before we reach the finish line. Except there is an infinite amount of this stuff and we can only carry what we can hold in our arms.

Douglas Adams, in *The Hitchhiker's Guide to the Galaxy*, says that 'humans are miserable pretty much of the time'. His electronic book, with 'DON'T PANIC!' written on the cover in bold red lettering, ascribes this fact to those little pieces of paper called money. Greed, or craving more things, and aversion, fear of losing those things, would seem to be the root of all our ills. But the thing we desire most in the world is immortality, and the thing we try to avoid at all cost is death.

This fear of death forces discontent upon us, aggravating negative traits: envy, self-loathing, cowardice and hatred. So, it seems the ultimate paradox of human existence, the fear of death, coerces us into thinking we are not handsome enough, not wealthy enough, not tall enough, not thin enough, simply not good enough. 'Something undesirable has happened, a desirable thing has not happened; mind becomes agitated,' explained S.N. Goenka, the Burmese Vipassana meditation rock star.

The illusion that we are never going to die becomes a habit of the mind. This pattern must be broken if we are to be free from the subconscious fear of death. Unless we break the habit of believing we are immortal, we will always be unhappy. We will forever have this nagging fear and self-doubt. It is fear of death, fear of the great change that clouds our vision of reality. There is a rule Benedictine monks live by which we could all do well to heed: that to live properly, monks should have death before their eyes at all times. This is a natural state for most climbers. And, having death before our eyes while rock climbing, day in, day out in wild nature, we can bring changes to our psyches that force us to see the ultimate reality of the world around us, our universe.

One of these realities is impermanence. Impermanence is the reality of everything, something the Buddha understood two and a half thousand years ago. When we examine our bodies, our minds, our thought processes, we grasp in vain to come up with anything that is permanent. All inanimate and animate objects are impermanent. Rocks and mountains weather and create soil, water evaporates and condenses to fall on land thousands of miles away, great trees fall down and in their place new life germinates. Animals, human and non-human, are born, age and die. We are each but one of 108 billion who have walked upon this Earth since the evolution of humanity, in one vast cycle of birth, life and death.

If we cling to permanence when in reality there is nothing that is permanent, we are headed for a lifetime of discontent. The ever-burgeoning cosmetic surgery business is proof of this the world over. Everyone wants to look like a Hollywood star. Everyone, it seems, desires eternal youth, as evidenced by the plethora of anti-ageing creams; billions are spent researching therapies to keep us young. If we are always chasing rainbows, believing that we are immortal, we will always be discontented, frustrated and not fully living. Alfred, Lord Tennyson was cognisant of death's vital inevitability. 'Old men must die; or the world would grow mouldy, would only breed the past again.' Only when we come to terms with our mortality, really study death's cold face, will we begin to lose our fear of it. And only then can we truly begin to live.

Lead climbing is one way to come to terms with our mortality. When we lead climb, we take certain risks and can't avoid the feeling of just how frail we are. We are vulnerable to injury, to mortality. To lead a climb is very different to seconding (to climb second means having the rope above you). Still, to climb second is exhilarating:

high up on a vertical wall, tying yourself in knots, making impossible moves. For the most part, this exciting routine takes place in complete safety. And seconding is an important step, if you intend to follow the winding path of The Mountain, to become proficient at climbing before moving on to lead.

On the sharp end of the rope, we are more readily forced to face and accept our fears: fear of heights, fear of falling and smashing ourselves up; fear of the unknown that is out in front of us. With the acceptance of this fear, we learn to live a courageous life. And courage is important if we are to let life's inevitable turbulence wash over us.

However, one must beware not to morph this courage into simple rashness, as I myself have been guilty of at times. The great existentialist psychologist Rollo May thought such bravado is only a display of one's unconscious fear, and 'getting one's self killed, or at least one's head battered in ... are scarcely productive ways of exhibiting courage'.

When I was in my twenties I enjoyed knocking about the Dinorwig slate quarries that towered above my home in Llanberis. I was drinking whisky in the Padarn Lake Hotel with Gwion Hughes, who I was living with at the time, when suddenly I had a smart idea.

'I have an excellent new climb to do. Why don't we go climbing?'

The pair of us swayed and staggered up to the vast Rainbow Slab. The climb I had seen was a long hairline fracture splitting the left side of the slab. And I had the misguided notion to climb it on sight, without pre-inspection from a rope – and a little bit intoxicated.

I threw a string of micro-wires, tiny brass-headed nuts, in the seam, without the least regard for my safety. The climbing was really quite difficult and became increasingly so. Nevertheless, I carried on with scant regard for my personal safety. I still remember attempting to pull on a depression into which you could place flat a fifty-pence piece: a strange, white pocket in a sea of blue-grey slate. I studied it for what seemed like an eternity and searched for my next hold. My shoe edges were set on mere ripples in the featureless slab. I began to slip and then accelerated down the slab, taking a twenty-five-metre fall.

The rope burned through the lycra behind my knee. I came to a halt inches from the ground.

So, being courageous and accepting fear doesn't in any way mean we should not be concerned for our own welfare. At the risk of seeming pretentious, let us call this technique of lead climbing to face our anxieties Fear Therapy. This is very different to the well-known Exposure Therapy, which recommends facing one's fears in relative safety and comfort. The term Exposure Therapy was coined in 1967 by psychologist Thomas Stampfl. It is also known as Flooding and is used today for treating a variety of anxiety disorders. It is a Pavlovian sort of behaviour therapy based on classical conditioning. If you are scared of dirty great spiders you are made to face dirty great spiders, though in safety, under glass and, by and by, you are systematically desensitised.

If you're scared of heights, then the act of climbing with a rope above you would make very good Exposure Therapy. In Australia there is a form of Exposure Therapy called Bush Adventure Therapy (BAT) for people affected by trauma and for people with various disabilities. It is having astounding results. Fear Therapy is not about curing psychological disorders, though many psychological disorders have been cured in this way. Young offenders are often encouraged to take climbing courses to get them on the right track again.

Back in the 1960s, behavioural therapist Joseph Wolpe conducted a rather extreme experiment, which admirably demonstrated 'flooding'. Wolpe took a girl who had a phobia of cars and sat her in the passenger seat (presumably without a seatbelt). He then drove her around the streets of New York for hours. In the beginning the girl was visibly hysterical, shaking, screaming and sweating, but she eventually relaxed when she realised that her situation was safe. From that day on she felt comfortable in cars. These days, happily, one can't go around kidnapping young girls and taking them for drives against their will, but Crazy Joe did just that and found it worked a treat.

In contrast, Fear Therapy works by directly confronting our fears in a real-time risk situation. Also, it must be said, Fear Therapy is not about curing an individual phobia, except perhaps for thanatophobia, the fear of death: our human condition. Its chief concern is building our acceptance levels, acceptance of all things. The acceptance of all things includes facing our fears and confronting the ultimate, or what Martin Heidegger called 'being towards death.' This encourages us to live an authentic life and teaches us how to confront these situations instinctively, without overthinking them. The Mountain teaches us to know intuitively what to do in the face of change.

When events take a sudden turn for the worse, every one of us will be faced with despair. When a long-term relationship goes pear-shaped, we will be filled with anguish. When all our valuable possessions are burgled, we will be despondent: 'What is the world coming to?' When someone close to us dies, we will be faced with unknowable loss. I argue that we can develop a capacity for turning these unfortunate events into a positive force for betterment. That risking our lives on a regular basis, facing our worst nightmare, death, in the mountains, does just this. It eases our despair because we will be in the process of becoming less attached to ourselves. Knowing that everything and everyone changes, has its season, is born and dies, then becomes a great release. We become free of the tremendous burden death loads upon us.

We know we can't avoid risk: risk to our bodies, financial risk, risk of bereavement, change –and yes, the risk of death. The great change, the one that British Orientalist Sir John Woodroffe called 'the high surgery of death', is an inherent and essential part of life. We may just as well attempt to hold our breath for the rest of our lives, which we know is impossible. It is out of the scope of this book to address the role of the state and the liability culture that we in the western world now live within. Suffice to say that we are creating a whole generation of kids who don't know how to take risks, can't see risks, and so end up killing themselves before they have begun living.

If everybody must face danger, stress, loss and bereavement, then we may as well learn how to do it properly. Lead climbing, or Fear Therapy, can teach us how to do it. Mark Twain said, 'Do the thing you fear most and the death of fear is certain.' (Or was it Ralph Waldo Emerson? Gautama Buddha probably said it first.) Whether it be a problem with intimacy, trusting people, anger issues, an overarching discontent with how things are, whether you are struggling with confidence or aimlessness or because you have found yourself caught in the very common trap of wanting more and more stuff – all these pains ultimately stem from fear of death. Fear Therapy, the simple act of leading a climb, can teach us how to trust and love, be committed to and content with the world. The more often we tie into the rope, the more often we face The Mountain, the deeper will be the imprint on our plastic brains.

In the history of brain science, neuroplasticity is a relatively recent concept. Many aspects of the brain can and will be altered by different activities and, if these activities are repeated often enough, a change in the wiring of the brain occurs. I have had direct experience of this cortical remapping, thanks to my brain injury in 1998, so feel well qualified to give advice. If every day we take a risk on the sharp end – not in an unbridled 'quest for experience' sort of way, but mindfully – our neural pathways *will* remap, and our brains *will* change. We will become less fearful and more courageous. But something further will happen. The defilements, as they are known by Buddhists, such as anxiety, anger, jealousy, greed and hatred, will slowly, one by one, lessen and ultimately disappear.

Gautama Buddha said: 'Mind precedes all mental states. Mind is their chief; they are all mind-wrought. If with an impure mind a person speaks or acts, suffering follows him, even as the wheel follows the foot of the ox.'

In effect, this means that the impure or negative mind will create suffering. It follows, then, that if we build up our courage, our suffering will lessen and at last cease, like a line carved in stone takes an age to scratch, deeper and deeper into the mind. Similarly, it takes a similar age to grind the stone smooth again, to restore the mind. Buddha seems to have learnt this neuroplasticity thing over 2,500 years ago.

'Here is a small fact. You are going to die,' says The Devil at the start of Markus Zusak's novel *The Book Thief*. Death will come and at any time. We must be prepared for it. Yes, we can get our funeral arrangements in order. We can have the songs we want our friends and family to listen to on the day pre-recorded. We can give instructions of how we want our corpse disposed of, and who we want to look after our house, our dog, our kids when we are gone. However, all this is of little importance if we can't accept the fact, truly accept the fact that this frail body we inhabit will wither and die. As Henry Wadsworth Longfellow wrote in his poem *Charles Sumner*, death 'stays our hurrying feet', and sooner than we think. Only when we have stayed our hurrying feet, and I certainly haven't yet, can we begin to live a life where courage takes precedence, where we can rationalise our fear and begin to transcend the material world.

5

DEATH

If I take death into my life, acknowledge it, and face it squarely, I will free myself from the anxiety of death and the pettiness of life – and only then will I be free to become myself.

– Martin Heidegger, *Being and Time*

Thoughts of my fall from Gogarth, the Welsh sea cliff, in 1993 have reached a tipping point recently. Powerful memories have mingled with insights that were invisible to me in the immediate aftermath.

You see, when I was twenty-six years old, I died. I fell into the sea and drowned. And my life was irrevocably altered, though it has taken the best part of three decades to work out in just what way. Because in dying you begin a journey of searching. In dying, your biography becomes your biology, so to speak.

I first wrote about my experience of death in *On the Edge* magazine in 1993. However, the way I wrote about it back then was with a spur-of-the-moment, as-it-happened immediacy. Now, from the vantage point of 2020, I see this event with crystal clarity as the most important experience of my life. The Totem Pole accident was to become my most treasured experience, but to actually die was wholly another matter.

Seen from the ferry that plies across the Irish Sea, Gogarth is a long turreted line of white and red teeth: like an infected jaw. These sea cliffs on the coastline of Ynys Môn hold a special place in the hearts of climbers in North Wales. Glenn Robbins and I were planning to climb the back wall of the deep white gash that is Wen Zawn, at Gogarth. Several years before Glenn and I ventured down there, Pat Littlejohn, a superb climber of the generation before mine, had created a direct start to a route in Wen Zawn called *The Games Climbers Play*.

This climb was the first to breach the overhanging cave at the very back of this monstrous feature in the Welsh coastline. It appeared to be steep enough and a worthy challenge, so we were keen to attempt a second ascent. Although when I say we, Glenn, my Australian photographer friend, had little interest in climbing that day and I had to plead with him, over several cups of tea in the cafe, to come with me. Eventually he acquiesced and at last we found ourselves abseiling down crumbling rocks into the depths of the inlet. Once at sea level I gazed up. The rock architecture of Wen Zawn is such that it acts as a natural fisheye lens, a wide angle for the mind.

Rock-hopping on boulders embedded in this cranny of the Irish Sea, we crossed the zawn and reached the wall opposite. Then we sat on a ledge just above sea level to survey our surroundings. Looking up at the route of the climb, I studied it closely and chose my gear carefully. Each fissure is a different size and will accept protection from brass nuts no bigger than a splinter of gravel to cams the size of a fist. Glenn uncoiled the rope. I tied in and rubbed the soles of my shoes until they were free of dirt, sticky and black.

'Okay, Glenn?'

'Right you are.'

The climb begins with a Stonehenge-like pillar and I rested at the top of this, about nine metres up. I placed a nut and a cam that would hold a falling bus and then set off through a system of small overhangs, content in what was for me a familiar environment. About ten metres higher I fiddled in two small nuts. My arms were beginning to tire. Littlejohn had given this direct start a grade of E4, which was well within my ability. I wasn't being overconfident; I knew Pat well and had climbed other routes of his graded up to E6 and had not overly struggled on them. I was going at this climb foreseeing an easy fight.

One horizontal overlap followed another.

By the time I had got through the third overhang, my forearms were swollen solid and pink with blood. Becoming anxious, I reached around yet another overhang, blind, and found the belay ledge; I was to fetch Glenn up from here. Getting on to it was another matter. It was sloping and water was trickling down the natural gutters worn in the stone. I matched my hands and because the wall was so steep, my feet naturally swung out from the rock. The face overhung so much that I remember pawing at the rock with my feet in a vain attempt to keep some form of contact. Glenn was shouting words of encouragement to me from twenty-five metres below. I attempted to mantelshelf on to the ledge by placing the butt of my hand and, with my elbow toward the wall, trying to press down. Nothing doing. The water trickled over my hands as I tried the move again. And again. Still nothing.

Soon enough I could see my efforts were futile. The chalk on my hands had turned to toothpaste on the wet hold. My arms had, I estimated, about another minute in them, but a minute is a long time in such a situation. I hung there on straight arms for what seemed an age, considering the best course of action. A metre and a half below my waist I had a good nut in, although small, about the thickness of the two fifty-pence pieces jingling around in my pocket. One metre below this was a more substantial aluminium nut: the dimensions of my thumb knuckle in a good V slot. Below that was more good gear. I felt safe enough to let go.

I would shout down to Glenn to 'take me' and make a controlled fall, four metres at the most, on to the small nut.

Okay, time and fingers were running out.

'Glenn?'

'Yeah?'

'Take us there.'

'Right.'

I let go.

First thing, the wire on the little nut sawed down a sharp edge of quartzite and snapped, though not before lifting out the other pieces when the rope went tight around the overhangs. This I should have foreseen by using longer quickdraws, or slings, to lessen the drag. I accelerated on down towards Glenn and on impact broke my tibia on the sharp, uneven rocks.

And this was just the beginning.

A moment later, I had somersaulted into a narrow, half-submerged, V-shaped cleft, dislocating both my shoulders and fracturing an acromion and my skull to boot. I had fallen thirty metres and was now upside down with my head underwater.

Glenn had to extricate himself from his belay and scramble down to me, a process that took around ten minutes. Luckily, he's a big man, and grabbing my ankles, he pulled me out of the cleft and tossed me over his shoulder. Then he clambered back up to the platform above the high-tide level and laid me down on my back. I had the certain memory of Glenn telling me he had once been a lifeguard on the beaches of Australia, so he would know the drill even if he'd only practised it on a lifeless dummy, which is effectively what I was. Years later I discovered this was a false memory. He had never been a life-guard, but he did know the rudiments of saving a person's life, and for this I'm very thankful.

First Glenn checked for a pulse. He couldn't find one.

'He was dead,' he later wrote. 'There was blood everywhere. His face was pale with a peaceful expression, and his eyes were rolled back in his head.'

There was no sign of breath either. The body that had been called Paul a few moments earlier was, to all intents and purposes, dead.

Around the same time, though it is difficult to be precise, I was having the most profound experience of my life. I was lying in a warm garden, in long grass, with insects buzzing. The light was slowly fading.

Back then I wrote that this had been 'the most beautiful part of all my life. Utterly final.'

The hallucination in my mind was fading from twilight to black. I was more than happy like this. As I wrote at the time, 'The tide could come in, night could fall, a storm could blow in from the west. I could slip out of my own back door and never return.' Finally, I was left in a dense, black, echoey space. I was standing in what felt like an empty football stadium, right in the centre of the pitch with the roof shut and the floodlights off.

In a state of despair, Glenn began mouth-to-mouth. Nothing happened. Then he frantically began pumping my chest. My eyes suddenly opened and I witnessed a jet of seawater hosing from my mouth, like the vomit scene in *The Exorcist*. That was when the pain began. Oh shit, I was alive again. I was fucking alive again. I had lost the most perfect moment of my life and come back to the torture of being alive. There were stabs of agony, like a blunt knife forcing its way between my ribs, into my lungs. It was almost too hard to bear. More than anything I wanted to go back to that dark place. But the old self-preservation system rose to the surface once again. The old *I* entered the room. *My* life needed saving. *My* self (*my* ego) had to be rescued. And luckily Glenn was right there.

As I writhed in pain, I noticed a blurry version of Glenn, as though seen through a watery fog, attempting to solo climb the sheer wall of the zawn, out of the predicament I had put him in. It was the only way he could see us being rescued. Lucky for him he failed, since it was now gently raining and the rock was wet. Otherwise he may have been added to the casualty list that dull afternoon.

Just then, as if a miracle, a lone figure appeared at the clifftop. Glenn relayed the urgency of our situation to him. His name was Ollie and he was a fellow climber from Llanberis. He ran and alerted the rescue services. An hour later I was in a helicopter being flown to the accident and emergency department in Bangor.

I spent a few weeks in hospital with all sorts of injuries, but a few months later I was back on the rock like nothing had happened. A fog often invaded my mind due to the assault on my brain, and I was receiving regular acupuncture on my aching shoulders. Other than that, I simply carried on my climbing life, albeit with a renewed vigour: a vigour approaching a death wish. I wasn't aware of it at the time, but I wanted nothing more than to lie down in that summer-evening garden again. I longed for that comfortable warm feeling, and searched for it through copious amounts of liquor and other drugs. Luckily for me, that serene vision, that enveloping garden was nowhere to be found. Within a year I had regained my own version of a wonky equilibrium and filed Wen Zawn in my personal mind-library of transgressions. My subconscious had found a new determination to survive. Not even on the Totem Pole, years later, did I let death into my living space (although I could sense him lurking at my door and wiping his feet on the welcome mat).

If I had died in that fall and Glenn hadn't managed to bring me back, I became convinced, back then, that part of me, my chi, my life current, would always have been part of Wen Zawn. I would have inhabited the quartz like a ghost. I would have been among the waves confusedly crashing into that parabolic gulf. I would have saturated the damp foreboding air of Wen Zawn. I see this now as overly romantic. It was how I would have liked things to have been and not how they were.

There were no lights at the end of tunnels. No looking down at myself on the sea-washed floor of the zawn. Nor did the memories of my life flash before my eyes, the types of event often recounted by others brought back in such situations. There was simply nothing out there. Nothing over the horizon. Nothing in that void. The light just extinguished slowly until I was left in that vast echoing space, still warm but utterly black. Somehow welcoming yet impersonal at the same time. Impersonal like a house might be when you really look at it, as simply bricks and mortar. But it gave me an immense solace. I wrote that I simply 'slipped into blackness'. I had no feelings of loneliness: in fact, just the opposite. I had the overwhelming sense that I was going home. The experience was not frightening; the darkness seemed to be welcoming me. I didn't read too much into this in the immediate aftermath of my accident, when I wrote about my plunge in *Deep Play*. But now I see that I was returning to my cosmic origins. I was coming home to myself.

As the years have gone by, I have become somewhat preoccupied by death; some might say unhealthily so, although I would disagree. Like Don Juan Matus, that real or imagined figure in the Carlos Casteneda books, I have been keeping 'death over my shoulder' since 1993. Very few people have direct experience of their own death. Few of the great philosophers who have theorised about the nature of death have done so with direct experience of what it is like to die, what it means to die, what becomes of the self when we die. But it is through the revelation I experienced at Gogarth that I have cemented my own beliefs on these things. And on how death has a bearing on how we live out our lives, and how we can make the most of our lives in the face of death's finality.

So much of our fear of death is ego-driven. The 'I' is terrified of death. And the consumer culture we have built for ourselves plays to that fear, if all you've ever thought about since you were a baby is the 'I' that feels good or the 'I' that feels hurt. The 'I' that wants that video game, the 'I' that doesn't feel rich enough. Or the 'I' that can't afford the fantasy house or car, just yet. So, we work longer hours at the office or the bank to be able to afford all this stuff. We are so busy that very few of us have the time to contemplate death, or anything else for that matter. Most of us are locked into punishing work schedules just to buy groceries and look after our families.

Add to this the medical approach to death that we in the western world (and an increasing number in the east also) have adopted in recent decades. We tend to save lives at all costs, even if the stricken person doesn't want their life saving. It is not unusual in many hospitals to deny a human a compassionate death, albeit through a form of well-intentioned over-treatment. We try at all costs to eke out life to the last possible moment. The end of a natural lifespan is often a drawn-out affair, taking weeks or months, even years. Very few family members or friends have the staying power or financial support to sit by their fading sister or father. Connected to all those tubes, stuck with needles, with a snorkel stuck down our trachea, we are robbed of the most important time in our lives: our precious last moments on the Earth, when we might be held by the ones we love or go on the last leg of this incredible journey in a forest or on The Mountain.

That the western world has forgotten how to die has been written about countless times and I don't wish to dwell on it. And I know dying connected to drip stands and monitors might be the right path for a limited number of people, but surely the majority of us would rather die with our dignity left intact? We have reduced this incredible journey, from birth, through a childhood full of wonder, to fierce adolescence, through our precarious twenties and thirties to well-rounded middle age, and old age filled with reflection, to what? An on–off button? We treat cattle in much the same way.

Western ideas of death have morphed through the centuries. In fourteenth-century England, life expectancy at birth was barely thirty. Even if you made it past childhood to twenty-five, you still only had another twenty-three years to go. Violence and plague were rife, and death was as much a part of life as birth. People understood that life was extraordinarily precious, and precarious. People understood that death was normal, but the promise of eternal life and an end of suffering through the intervention of Jesus Christ was possible. By the twentieth century, death had become a taboo subject and the chief enemy of humanity, just as Christianity rolled back from its high-water mark. The moment of death was moved from the home to the hospital, accelerating the era of what French death historian Philippe Ariès calls the 'forbidden death'.[1] Throughout my childhood and my teens, relatives and friends were dying, and yet the first

---

1   *Western Attitudes Toward Death from the Middle Ages to the Present*, Philippe Ariès, 1974.

corpse I ever saw was aged twenty-six on the Trango glacier in Pakistan.

Now, in the twenty-first century, death has come to be almost shameful in western society. Many more people die out of sight than in any other period in history. A child does not learn about death and rarely witnesses it, and if they do they are likely to be sent for counselling. The denial of death is no less evident than the search for immortality, which has been seriously ramping up these past decades. In the process, we are denying people the opportunity to die with compassionate presence, although friends working in the field tell me the situation is beginning to change, albeit slowly. We certainly need a new way of dying. Take it from someone who's been there.

Buddhist and Hindu approaches to death seem more positive. In chapter 2 of the *Bhagavad Gita*, Arjuna is about to go into battle in his chariot. He sees relatives and friends amongst the ranks of the enemy and begins to despair, 'How shall I strike my grandfather, my guru, and all other relatives?' Krishna turns to Arjuna and tells him plainly, 'I have never not existed; nor have you, nor have these lords of men. Nor will we cease to exist, all of us, from now onwards.' And that crazy, gun-toting god-man Osho, the 'Rolls-Royce guru', said, 'If there is no end there can be no beginning.' And, of course, these devotees recognise various forms of rebirth and reincarnation, life and death in an eternal cycle.

But we don't have to believe in any kind of afterlife in a traditional sense to grasp the idea that humans are part of a whole. If all life is part of one system, as it appears in Arne Naess' *Deep Ecology* philosophical model, every part of the universe is linked to every other part in one eternal flow. This means that we never truly die. I have already argued in this book that we really are immortal. How our physical matter, the billions of cells of our bodies, goes back out into the universe. To be reincarnated as a particle of a moth's wing, to be eaten by birds of the future. Or to break as a wave on a distant planet's shoreline. Or to become a white speck on a saxifrage flower in an alpine pasture, in the shadow of The Mountain. In this sense, we will never die.

Having said all this, I was recently gazing at the clouds as they morphed into different shapes – ostrich, python, broom, anvil, Om symbol, hammer and sickle – daydreaming, as you do. I suddenly realised that I wanted to be part of those clouds. In a sense I wanted to die. I wasn't suffering from depression. I wasn't lonely or crying for help. I was sober.

I do think that Ernest Becker was right on the nose with his death anxiety thesis (we all want to avoid death).[2] However, I believe we are also fascinated by death and instinctively desire to go back to the one, to be at one with the fabric of the universe. But rightfully we are terrified of *the* big change. To me, this is the great dilemma of life.

Added to this, it is true, science does not yet have the answer for what becomes of our consciousness when we die. And, let's face it, as individuals we are only our consciousness. Sure, we have our bodies (for now), but my journey through disability has proved to me that our physical being is immaterial. Our consciousness makes our reality in an 'if a tree falls in the forest' kind of sense. I like to think when we expire our consciousness returns to the universal mind, or a fundamental layer of reality, in a panpsychist view of reality. To me this universal mind is more simply known as God. It is Allah, Brahma, Baiame. It is the over-soul, the universal spiritual force encoded in our DNA.

This return to our 'maker' surely makes our 'death day' as important as our birthday, and no less worthy of celebration. They are both moments of ultimate change. Death is the great landmark of our lives, a voyage that can go by in the blink of an eye if you let it. It has taken me these long years since my fortuitous death to understand that we should celebrate our death. This human life into which we are born is a precious gift, but it took falling and drowning that murky day at Gogarth to make me realise this. No other animal can appreciate a poem or go bowling, read a great novel or bake a fantastic loaf of bread. Added to this jewel of a life, the chances of us being born

---

2   Ernest Becker, *The Denial of Death*, 1973.

as our unique selves and not some other random collection of matter are incomprehensibly small. So why not celebrate a life 'dancing with the angels?'

Death is also the culmination of everything we have done throughout our lives, good and bad. Simply, the interior knowledge that you at least attempted to be kind throughout your life will at the moment immediately before death bring you peace. For our deeds, good or bad, will carry karma beyond our earthly life. I'm not talking about being reborn as a slug or a saint. I'm talking about how non-violent or violent speech or actions have consequences beyond the grave.

On a much lesser scale, we may hate our neighbour for a number of years and she in turn might hate us. When we die, the hate we encouraged when we were alive *will* keep on being precipitated through others. The moments preceding our death, if we accept these moments, can be a time of ultimate forgiveness and reconciliation: one final act of compassion and empathy before slipping back to our cosmic origins.

One final lesson that falling to my death taught me was radical acceptance. How to let go of what I most desired in life: life itself. With this acceptance I learnt how, moment by moment, to let go and simply accept what is. All of it, all the time. In this way, I am able to trust my intuitions (most of the time) and accept things as they really are. With radical acceptance we can also be non-judgemental of those around us who may be losing their heads. If we can truly accept everything around us, we can then accept that we are not in control of our lives (though we would like to think that we are). Most importantly, we let go of this railing against reality and just acknowledge that this is the way it is going to be from here on in.

You may think this sounds like giving up on life. But I don't think radical acceptance of the way things are precludes our attempts at righting the many wrongs in the world. We are still right to go out and protest against human rights violations and oceans full of garbage. We only radically accept the moment that we are in, and what is gone.

We still have the ability to change the next moment, and change it we will, for better or worse (hopefully better). The Vietnamese Buddhist monk Thich Nhat Hanh wrote, 'The present moment is the only moment available to us, and it is the doorway to all moments.' Allowing this, we can tolerate the present moment, however excruciatingly painful. And, as no one knows when their time will be up, having an attitude of acceptance towards death welcomes one into the vast family of all living beings. For all beings live and die. They come and go.

Even so, accepting our own death is one thing. Those who are left behind are another matter. They are often devastated to the point of illness. How would my family have dealt with my death had it occurred permanently that day in Wen Zawn? After my brain injury on the Totem Pole, my mother contracted breast cancer. Was that connected to her worry over my health? She certainly thought so. Loved ones left behind grieve, and they are right to do so. Grief is natural. I have been to more young climbers' funerals than I care to mention. These deaths are hard on the families of those who are gone. The lives of some people, especially climbers, seem unusually ephemeral. They are like a flower that passes in an unseasonal frost. Each one of us is as impermanent as spring snowfall, and everything in our lives is fundamentally unpredictable. No one knows when they are going to die. Would it not then be possible for families to radically accept the deaths of loved ones too? Death is around us every day and those who have lost someone close must know that their friend, mother or brother has simply gone back home, to the one. With this knowledge, there is reason to celebrate a life well lived, however short.

Thinking about death all the time, as I am prone to do, can seem to put the dampers on life. However, I often argue that contemplating our demise is essential if we are to make the most of our lives. As the existential psychiatry pioneer Irvin Yalom said, 'existence cannot be postponed'. To live a full life, we must intimately know our limitations, the profoundest of which is not knowing how long we have got clinging to this rock we call Earth. Our life is the greatest first ascent we will ever do. Don't look to that other ridge thinking you have chosen the wrong route. The way above may look difficult, but you have chosen the plumb line. Sure, you may have to traverse diagonally to the side now and again to avoid certain obstacles. But you just need to try your very best on this section of your climb, right here, right now.

When we face death, we know we are alive. Thus, we see that we are part of eternity. In that moment of death, I saw that I had lived a life groping in the dark. Until I died, I did not know beauty. Not truly. I did not know bliss. I did not feel awe.

Until I died.

6

STILLNESS

And men go abroad to admire the heights of mountains, the mighty billows of the sea, the broad tides of rivers, the compass of the ocean, and the circuits of the stars, yet pass over the mystery of themselves without a thought.

— St Augustine, *Confessions*

The Cordillera Real, Bolivia. I awoke to a freezing night. The beam of my headlamp illuminated curious ice roses, created by frost on the tussocks of grass about my sleeping bag, laid out in an alpaca pen. Up above stood silhouetted the south face of El Ala Izquierda del Condoriri.[1] The night sky was a mass of Van Gogh stars, and meteoroids sparking as they entered the planet's atmosphere. In the absence of a tent, the constellations of Cassiopeia, Crux del Sur and Triangulum Australis were framed above me. The mighty diamond of Sirius glowed and warmed my face. Well, it seemed to. I turned off my headlamp and lay back, hands behind my head, and quite unexpectedly welled up.

Those who know me are aware that since the Totem Pole I tend to pile exhausting layers of complexity on to any event. I will extrapolate any simple thing, such as doing some gardening, to its logical philosophical conclusion. 'By planting this lettuce seedling am I

---

1   El Ala Izquierda del Condoriri means 'the left wing of the condor'.

metaphorically laying the groundwork for change: letting go of the past and embracing the future? Or am I attempting to distract myself from my ultimate fate – death – as a form of terror management of my existential dread?' Except that this extraordinary night on the Altiplano was long before that rock fell on my head. It was 1990 and I was twenty-three years old.

All of us who have slept out under the Milky Way have experienced this awe. And while I don't think we can simply put such feelings down to the incomprehensible vastness of the cosmos, it is nevertheless staggering that if we were to travel at the speed of light, we would loop the Earth seven times in a second. And that travelling at this speed it would take four hours to reach Neptune. Four years to reach Proxima Centauri, our nearest star. Twenty-five thousand years to reach the Canis Major Overdensity, our nearest galaxy. Eleven million years to the ESO 540-030 galaxy in the Sculptor Group. And 32 billion years to reach GN-z11, the most distant object yet seen in the universe.[2]

Absolutely all of us have had epiphanies of this kind at some point or other. These existential feelings of insignificance are part of the human condition. The tiny-speck-of-dust feeling that seems to convey that in the grand scheme of things we do not matter.

The temptation to be overcome for a few minutes, half an hour at most, prevails. We might even sob. Then it is put back into some dusty recess of the mind in order to preserve our sanity. That night in the Cordillera, looking up into the night sky, I did have such an experience of insignificance, how it would be easy to think that humans don't matter, that we are irrelevant in this universe of great cosmic events and unknowable distances.

Obviously, I think we do matter. We matter as much as anything else in the universe because we are the universe. And the universe is us. We are all made up of the same gaseous compounds as the dusty

2   Even though the universe is only 13 billion years old, the rate of expansion means it would take 32 billion years to reach GN-z11.

Milky Way that looms overhead. Each and every one of our bodies is as void and empty as the spacious night sky. We are made up of the same stuff as The Mountain, and the snow upon it. Our bodies might feel solid and tangible, but each of us is an empty house.

That night, the back of my head cradled in my hands, I felt the freedom and solidarity that only comes with the knowledge that everything is contained in the one, and the one is contained in everything. I convulsed. Tears streamed down my face. You might think I was weeping at the sheer beauty of it all, the vastness of the cosmos combined with the raw simplicity of that which lay above me. Like countless millions before me, I was having one of those 'the universe is really massive and I am insignificant in it' moments. Perhaps I was. Yet that wasn't the only reason I was so overcome with emotion that bitter night, although at the time I only had an inkling of why I was sobbing so painfully. It took eight years and the Totem Pole accident to work it out.

I had previous experience of this dissolution of ego, this psychological singularity, rare moments as a kid in the mountains of Scotland, England and Wales when I had become similarly absorbed into the landscape. These revelations occurred more deeply later, when I started rock climbing. Half-glimpsed insights, like seeing a face at the front door through frosted glass: watching my own body climb a sea cliff; time slowing to a standstill during a particularly long fall from a slate quarry near my home in Gwynedd. Later, after that rock had destroyed my ability to do the complex gymnastics The Mountain demands, I would experience the same perspective of reality during meditation.

I like thought experiments and one of the most famous involves Albert Einstein, Boris Podolsky and Nathan Rosen. It's called the EPR paradox. Together, the three physicists demonstrated that the theory of quantum mechanics thus far was incomplete. The behaviour of a particle in what is known as an entangled pair did not adhere to the laws of physics and was, as Einstein put it, 'spooky'. One of the pair seemed to know what measurement had been performed on the other, even though a considerable distance (in quantum terms) separated the two particles.

The EPR paradox was meant to expose the flaws in quantum theory, but is now fundamental to quantum mechanics, demonstrating how a particle violates the laws of classical physics. I believe this paradox also illustrates how all matter is empty in a Buddhist sense – that is, like with the entangled particles, in a dependent origination sense. The EPR paradox shows how everything that exists is dependent on other extant factors – that we are, in effect, one interconnected indivisible whole.

In 1950 Einstein wrote a letter of consolation to Rabbi Robert S. Marcus, political director of the World Jewish Congress. Marcus had witnessed the liberation of Buchenwald and helped hundreds of desperate young boys he discovered there find safe passage to France. He campaigned at the United Nations for stateless people, and was on his way to France to continue this work when he discovered that three of his children had contracted polio. By the time he made it home to New York, his eleven-year-old first-born son, Jay, had died. In his grief, the rabbi wrote to Einstein seeking consolation. Einstein wrote back a letter of immense insight that was just three sentences long and began:

A human being is part of a whole called by us 'Universe', a part limited in time and space. He experiences himself, his thoughts and feelings, as something separate from the rest – a kind of optical delusion of his consciousness.

This is, for me, the crux of the letter. Amongst certain philosophies of life, Buddhism being one, delusion or superstition is one of the three defilements that lead to suffering. Opposing delusion is wisdom. Einstein concluded his letter of condolence by writing, 'The striving to free oneself from this delusion is the one issue of true religion.' He was adopting a Buddhist stance, that 'form itself is emptiness, and emptiness itself is form', to quote the second verse of *The Heart Sutra*.[3] This emptiness must include the physical human body of the dead boy, recycled through the universe, as it has been countless times. Robert Marcus himself died just two years later, at the age of forty-one.

Einstein's theories of relativity are the basis of Alexander Friedmann's and Edwin Hubble's theories of an infinitely expanding universe, culminating in today's big bang theory. This theory proposes that every speck of matter in the hundreds of billions of galaxies each with at least a billion stars emerged from a unified field of pure energy, and from a space smaller than a single atom.

What is more, the entire universe today is still that unified field, along with all matter in it: the asteroids zooming throughout it, the countless solar systems, the soil and animals of the Earth. Us. We are simply a field of pure energy. Carl Sagan said, 'We are a way for the cosmos to know itself.' (And Joni Mitchell was channelling Sagan when she sang about us being stardust.) Every atom in our bodies is directly connected to every other atom in the universe. Every particle continues to be recycled and flow throughout the universe through a process known as Jeans escape.[4] A 1953 Smithsonian Institute experiment found that ninety-eight per cent of what makes us who (we think) we are was not there last year and will not be part of who we are next year. We are like the ship of Theseus, where every plank and spar had been changed several times.[5]

Only when I was camped on the Altiplano under Condoriri, entranced by the cold night and its stars, did I become cognisant of how empty of self I really was. How we are all of us every other single 'thing' in the universe. And like everything else, a process of becoming that never becomes.

---

3   Buddhist Text Translation Society, 1997.

4   Named after British astronomer Sir James Jeans, who first described the process of atmospheric loss.

5   The ship of Theseus was a philsophical conundrum written about by Heraclitus and Plato and picked up by Plutarch and then Hobbes. Was it the same ship? Or a different one? The Buddhist *Prajnaparamita Sutra* has a similar story, although it involves demons and a corpse.

A satellite slid across the night sky on an invisible track. My mind, wandering freely, settled on considering human consciousness. That satellite was designed by humans, a product of human consciousness. One of myriad inventions that continuously build on what has gone before, from animal skins to Gore-Tex jackets, from the first cooking fire to the hydrogen bomb. How many people did it take to build that satellite? From the design stage, quarrying raw materials, producing the gyroscopes and solar arrays? Tens of thousands, I would guess. Humans are smart individually, but together we are smarter.

On The Mountain we immerse ourselves completely in the natural world. And we have glimpses of an ultimate reality. One aspect of this submersion is a holistic worldview, that we experience a kind of oneness-of-all-things, which includes an individual's consciousness.

I don't think I'd heard of the concept of 'universal consciousness' as a twenty-three-year-old lad bivouacked under a Bolivian mountain, but there was clearly more happening here than simply dossing in an alpaca pen or climbing a tilted sheet of ice might initially reveal.

Philosophers from the ancient pre-Socratics and Plato right through to Hegel, Spinoza and Schopenhauer have held that all minds are connected in some way. This is more commonly called universal consciousness and sometimes, more controversially, panpsychism, the view that every physical thing is associated with consciousness. So the idea has a long tradition in western thought. More recently, neuroscientists Giulio Tononi and Christof Koch have espoused a form of panpsychism with their Integrated Information Theory of Consciousness (IIT).[6] Panpsychists tell us that in fact there is only one mind, one consciousness that each individual mind taps into to create her or his own consciousness; though other philosophers such as Roger Penrose, John Searle and Noam Chomsky have all implied that a revolutionary change in physics may be needed to solve the problem of consciousness. We are still some distance from understanding how consciousness arises; the Australian philosopher

6   IIT states that at every level of existence there is consciousness.

and cognitive scientist David Chalmers has called it the 'hard problem'.

Ever since I was a kid, scrambling with my mum on the Isle of Arran, I had been used to that crumb-of-dirt feeling you feel against the potency and grandeur of The Mountain. That only increased as I travelled to the greater ranges. Yet, as I blindly sensed that night, there is something else, beyond knowing we are just specks in the universe, something even more mystifying. It amazes me how much modern science doesn't know about the nature of reality. And nowhere is that demonstrated more than in the 'observer effect'.

The observer effect is well known and often it's quite banal. Checking your tyre pressure will change your tyre pressure, because a little of the air gets out. Sometimes it's nothing short of miraculous. The outcome of a quantum experiment, for example, can change depending on whether or not we choose to measure some property of the particles involved. In other words, whether anybody is watching. This is ingeniously demonstrated by the famous double-slit experiment where particles can behave as waves and waves as particles. Even weirder, passive observation of the experiment can change the measured result. The Schrödinger's cat thought experiment is a demonstration of the problem this wave-particle duality poses.[7]

In 2017 a similar experiment was taken into space and a single photon was fired thousands of kilometres to rebound off a satellite (not the satellite I observed from my alpaca pen, tracking across the darkness of space), with the same inconclusive result: the fact that the experiment was observed altered the result of it. Even the great Richard Feynman couldn't put his finger on the observer effect, claiming in a public lecture it was 'the only mystery of quantum mechanics'.[8] If we take this bizarre phenomenon to its logical

---

7   Schrödinger famously stated that if you place a cat and a radioactive atom in a sealed box, you would not know if the cat was dead or alive until you opened the box, so that the cat was both alive and dead until you did so.

8   *The Feynman Lectures on Physics, Volume 3*, Richard P. Feynman; Robert B. Leighton and Matthew Sands (1965). Addison-Wesley.

conclusion, it would suggest that rather than consciousness some-how arising out of our brains, matter arises out of consciousness. In a very real sense, we have always been here, in the universe, and will continue being here until the end of time (if such a time or place exists).

I think what I inferred from these experiments is that reality really is what you make of it. And, sleeping out on the icy ground in a remote valley in the Bolivian Andes, I felt I was living my reality to my utmost. In that moment in the Cordillera Real, not only did I feel one with The Mountain and the night, but I felt a connection to everyone on Earth. Each one of us is the Arab, the European, the Inuit of Frobisher Bay, the San of the Kalahari and the Pitjantjatjara of the Central Desert. We are all the Hindu, the Christian, the Muslim, the exis-tentialist and the Jew. We are the asylum seeker in the detention centre, and the Mexican child warehoused in the Texan desert. Closer to my heart, every one of us is that guy we just stared at in the wheelchair and thought we'd rather be dead than to end up like that.

What is more, we do not have a life: we *are* life. We have not had an infinite number of past lives; we have had every life, past, present and into the future.

We are not simply talking about humans either, but everything that has ever existed. As the climber and conservationist John Muir said, 'when we try to pick out anything by itself, we find it hitched to everything else in the universe'. We are the pilot whale stranded on the beach, and the people lovingly draping her in wet towels, we are the giant *Eucalyptus regnans* and the tiny bee hummingbird. We are the fossiliferous rocks of Chomolungma and, quite literally the Baltoro glacier (as we are made up of sixty-five per cent water). Most importantly, we are all my dog Pancho, which makes me very happy.

Of course, I also believe it is essential to feel insignificant before the night sky, wild nature, the mountain's bulk. That speck-of-dust feeling is vital if we are to know our true place in the universe. I really used to think I was someone. Now I saw the truth: I was just borrow-ing this body.

I thought about what I had said to Andy Pollitt after repeating his route *A Wreath of Deadly Nightshade*. How I hadn't thought it deserved the grade he had given it.

'It was more like E5!' I had said smugly.

I remembered as well the look he had given me.

'Oh, Paul.'

I had once dreamt of being a big player in the climbing world. I had imagined a life of fame for myself. Fortune could take a flying leap and I was never interested in riches. But now, I realised, I had been nothing but a hungry ghost: envy and jealousy had me in their throe.[9] And in this moment, reclining under that night sky in the Cordillera, I had an inkling of my true insignificance. That we are nothing. Although the realisation was still buried deep, I lay beneath the Milky Way and without knowing it joined the ranks of 'the everything'.

Now, years later I rejoice in my insignificance. My subconscious grasped, right there, under the slopes of Condoriri, that if I didn't do this, I would fall. Not take a physical fall down The Mountain: I was feeling too confident for that. No, the fall I mean is the metaphorical fall that all of us, bar a few, will take sooner or later.

If we look at it rationally, we know we are not the greatest climber in the world. How can we be? We do not have the greatest mind. How could we? We are not God's gift to women or men or both. Advertisers would like us to imagine we could be any of these things. Craving sells nourishing herbal hydrolysing facial repair creams, fear sells cognitive training programmes and self-doubt sells ab-cruncher machines. Yet, we are never the greatest anything in the world. Not even close.

My mind was entering a feedback loop now. I had to get some rest. I pulled my arms inside my bag, took one last peek at Cassiopeia and drifted off to sleep. I awoke before dawn and turned on my headlamp. I retrieved my boots from inside my bivvy bag, where I'd stowed them so they wouldn't freeze. I rolled up my bag and stashed my kit in

---

9   A Buddhist concept, the hungry ghost, with a distended stomach and pinhole mouth, is used as a metaphor for greed. They are never satiated and forever craving.

a corner of the alpaca fold. Breath condensed in the torch beam as I picked my way through the talus to the foot of the tilted south flank of El Ala Izquierda del Condoriri.

As dawn broke I began my rhythmic pace up the ice face.

Later that morning, perched atop the summit of The Mountain, I could see every horizon. North along the spine of the Cordillera, I gazed down on Ch'iyar Quta, the 'black lake' to the south, then east to the Amazonas and Brazil, and west, to Titicaca.

For the briefest moment, I saw the big picture.

7

THE APPROACH

We should go forth on the shortest walk, perchance, in the spirit of undying adventure, never to return — prepared to send back our embalmed hearts only as relics to our desolate kingdoms. If you are ready to leave father and mother, and brother and sister, and wife and child and friends, and never see them again — if you have paid your debts, and made your will, and settled all your affairs, and are a free man — then you are ready for a walk.

— Henry David Thoreau, *Walking*

Come with me on this adventure. You're invited. You will lead the way. I will accompany you on the approach to the mountain ahead of us, the one in the middle distance. Once at the base, you will prepare your equipment with care and we will embark on the climb together.

* * *

We climb down from the vehicle halfway up the pass and step on to the metalled roadway. There are cars parked in the lay-by opposite the boulders. I watch you cross the road and grasp the lichenous timber 'X' of the stile. Stepping on to the first step, you are feeling anxious, although you can't put your finger on why. Your booted foot lingers for a moment on the road, photographically frozen, tiptoed on the tarmac ... then breaks free. You leave the everyday chitter-chatter on the metallic surface of the road, along with the litter, the white lines and the 'Give Way' signs. You briefly balance atop the wall and glance up at the clouds, cumulus all rushing in the same easterly direction.

On the other side of the wall, you step down softly on to a great expanse of moss. This carpet of moss seems to envelop you as you sink momentarily. This is it. The threshold crossed, you eye a suitable path. Across the glaciated valley, there are two ways. The low path looks muddy from too many feet. Up higher you eye a path that traverses a hillside and meets a scree slope in about a mile and a half. From the top of the scree you can see a patch of hard spring snow, and then the actual rock face of the mountain. It is a simple choice and you make it without conscious thought. You decide to keep your boots out of the sludge for as long as possible.

You pace for the Thoreauvian West, the land of opportunity. And like Thoreau, in the town where you live, your 'obligations to society' are still running around your head. Unlike Thoreau, you find value in society, in the urban existence. We must live in a house, unless one wishes to be like Diogenes and live in a barrel.

You begin your approach, attempting to remain weightless, so as not to disturb the green dewy carpet. A lark levitates from its nest, his melodic rush of song rising in and out of the wind. That bird brings a smile to your face. You turn silently about. I am right behind you.

You walk on. As you fit into your stride you become ever so slowly aware of an alertness. Like déjà vu. You are waking up. You have been here before. You are increasingly attentive to the sound coming from the landscape. A trickle of water. The strangled cry of some distant livestock. Your own footfall seems deafening. Then you hear it. A deep hum. You strain to discern whether the sound is coming from far away or nearby. It's not a car or plane, you're sure of that. Is it coming from the land? Your body? Your head? You can't fathom it. Not yet.

You walk on, feeling the weight of your clothes, the pack on your back. The stretch of your hamstrings. An aching stillness in your hands. You're arching your back. You feel the cool moistness of sweat when the damp rucksack is peeled off your shoulders. You are breathing heavily now as the path steepens. You feel the pulse of your heart. That mild headache you had when you left the road has all but dissipated.

These first stages of the walk-in bring to mind the first lines of a poem by R.S. Thomas.[1] It's about going up a track that you could drive in a motorcar, but is best walked slowly. You strain to put the words in the correct order, but then perform a kind of mental back-pedal, as you get the idea that any taxing of the mind will result in getting lost in worldly matters. It's something about taking note of the mosses and lichen that write history's calligraphy on the grey rock. Something about hearing the spinning of a nightjar's house. Its beauty isn't about the precise position of the words anyway. A poem's fascination must be contained in its ... oh not now.

You notice that you are alive. So alive. You're aware of a tingling in your legs and arms. Alert to the landscape around you, the world around you. You sense the orbital vibration of the billions of atoms that make up your body and all beings' bodies.

You go deeper.

As the narrow path gains altitude, you let your senses open wide like a delicate flower greeting the sun. The moss is disappearing, giving way to an alpine garden: the tiny cuneiform heads of saxifrage and the delicate bobbing white flowers of rock cress. The badger-faced sheep have nibbled the grass down to the quick, and rocks break the surface like schools of whales. You pick your way up the hill, listening carefully.

'That's it!'

You put the side of your head against an anvil-sized rock. You've got it. You can hear the woodlice underneath the stones on which you tread. This time you smile on the inside, with wonder.

Even though I keep three paces behind you, we walk in silence and solitude. You experience every footfall, in the present moment. Every

---

1   'Ninetieth Birthday'.

movement of the air, every minute difference in temperature: all in the present moment. Every odour. You smell the grass, the goats on the wind, the lichen on the rocks. The earth. The Earth. The anxiety you were experiencing when you set off from the roadhead has gone. It isn't even a memory. It is simply not there. The harsh words you used to your lover. You don't regret saying them and you aren't drowning in sorrow. What's said is said. What's done is done. You know you can't alter the past, but you can endeavour to make it right from here on in. You make a pact with yourself to pause before opening your mouth in future. You will talk it over with your lover when you get home.

In a similar way, as you climbed over that stile, you had a sense of dread rising from deep inside. You had an inkling it was about what the future holds. But you can't put your finger on it. You know you're going to get that redundancy note soon. Maybe that's it. And that this is putting stress on your relationship. So maybe that's it.

'What will become of us?'

Or is it bigger than that? You recently read how the world's eighty-five richest people own as much as the poorest fifty per cent of humanity. You recently saw images of a gyre of rubbish in the Pacific Ocean covering 1.6 million square kilometres. Or is your deep-seated worry bigger still? Melting icecaps. Deforestation. A global pandemic.

'What about the planet?' you were screaming silently. 'What … about … the … planet?'

But for now, it's just you and the next footfall. You and your next breath. Inhale … Exhale … You like the feeling of breathing. Inhale … Exhale … It makes you feel alive. Those are all problems. Inhale … Exhale … You realise that, and you will do as much as one person can do to make it right. Inhale … Exhale … Vote for equity, the planet. Use less stuff. Inhale … Exhale … But in this moment, you become an animal once again. Senses open and alert to the Earth. Inhale … Exhale …

There are two elements to the approach to The Mountain. There is the external world of forest, glacier and alpine moor. And the internal world, of bone mechanics, pulsing organs, straining ligaments: the workings of the body. The external world requires you to be alert, stealthy, like an animal, alive to every detail, however minute. The distant clink of another climber's hardware, the kestrel that faces the breeze as it hovers, the single droplet of water blown on to the back of your hand, its pleasant sting.

The internal workings of your body harmonise with the external senses in a balanced dance of the mind. Not only do you give your full attention to the earth, the smell of the earth, the sound of the earth, the touch of the earth; but with each breath you take, the outside world enters your body. You then use some of it, add some gases of your own and release it back into the outside world. External becomes internal ... Internal external.

You pay close attention to the beating of your heart as you steadily climb up the rising path. It is strong, regular and fast. Your tongue sticks to your palate through lack of saliva. You will take some water at the snow patch. You notice a twinge deep inside your hip joint. It's bordering on painful, but you know it will pass. You know any phenomenon comes and goes, presents itself and then fades away. Is born and dies.

The simple act of walking to The Mountain has become a meditation. When you walk, you pay attention to your feet, noticing how they strike the bare earth. 'When the past and the future can't pull you away anymore, every step is solid,' Thich Nhat Hanh said. You note whether your heel strikes first, or the ball of your big toe. It is the ball as we climb up the hillside. It will be a heel strike on the way back down. You compare your two feet. You are walking on the outside of your left foot. However, you are maintaining equal weight on each foot. You observe the relationship between your feet, pelvis, knees, ankles, spine and head as you walk. Shoulders and arms. You swing your right arm with your left leg (whereas I swing my right arm with my right leg). You are just paying attention to it. This is enough.

You approach the scree field with the monk's words in your mind. You eye the line we will take across the great apron of scree. You can make out a 'path': well-worn stones over which many feet have trod. Together we will follow this path. On the far side, about 500 metres away, is the shrinking remnant of a spring snowfield. We will aim for that.

First you pause to urinate, taking notice of the hot flush in your genitals. You watch the steam from your stream of piss as you feel the relief of your bladder deflating. As you do yourself up, a mildly astringent waft catches your nose.

'Am I peeing mindfully?' you ask yourself. And laugh.

You prepare to tiptoe across the scree slope, intricately poised blocks at an angle of about thirty-five degrees. This is the median angle of repose for this particular dolerite scree, brought down from the mountain face over thousands of years. You are keenly aware of just how ancient and present the landscape is. You are also aware of how dynamic it is. Forever changing. Moment to moment.

You enter this choppy sea of stone by putting your left boot on a plate of dolerite the dimensions of a paella pan. You position your foot on the left side of the paella pan, estimating this to be the most stable place to step without tipping the rock. The white-blotched plate holds fast as you make the half-second decision to put your right boot on the portable-TV-sized block just ahead of the paella pan.

You decide to see just how far you can walk without shifting a stone under your weight. The difficulty is dependent on the size, shape, texture and dampness of the individual rocks. Each has a tactile signature you discover through your boot sole, the texture judged haptically through the bottom of your boot. You imagine it's like feedback from a steering wheel in a driving video game. Then you gently reprimand yourself for lifting that video game over the stile. You tell yourself it should have stayed in the other world. The artificial one.

You begin to ponder 'dependent origination', how all phenomena arise from other, pre-existing phenomena. There's no danger of attempting to unpack a Buddhist concept right here, in the middle of this great, loose tsunami of scree. In fact, where better than in the middle of a huge, imperceptibly moving mass of rocks. The existence of that driving game is only possible through conditionality. Everything comes from something. The video game is powered by electricity, which is generated by, for example, coal, which originated in the ancient swamps and peat bogs of the Carboniferous Period, whose remnants include the mountain you are walking on today. The imaginary car in the game is projected on to a silicate glass screen, an amorphous solid roughly as impermanent as the rockslide you're teetering across right now.

If not dressed in wet lichen, and thus slimy, the large angular boulders are easy to trust. But they may still roll. Smaller, rounded rocks are almost impossible to judge, unless you happen to see that the stone has shifted recently. You notice one domestic-iron-shaped stone is not in the same position as it was until recently. You can tell by the pale line between the moss and the rock, which rests on another that's much larger. You step on it with extra care. It shifts about two millimetres, then holds. Moss fills the grykes and ankle-twisting holes, concealing their dangers, and curious hairy lichen grows on some blocks, which makes you pause.

You sneak on. You choose your stones with a burglar's gait, swag bag on your back. You treat walking across the scree as a further meditation. You imagine trying to walk over a dune of golf balls without one shifting. Impossible? Perhaps, but your efforts aren't altogether futile.

The autumn sun has been hiding behind the ridge but now is edging on to your face. You pause, mid-touch-and-go step, between an anvil and a *Roget's Thesaurus*, and close your eyes. You let the sun, our sun, warm your face, warm your mind, warm your heart. You are approaching the far edge of this drifting continent of scree and are content and surprised as to how few rocks shifted under the combined weight of you and your backpack.

At last you step down from the scree on to the snow patch. You take the pack off your back and, after retrieving a bottle and some chocolate, you sit on it. You put the bottle to your lips and feel, really feel, the icy water as it pours down your throat. You notice the coldness of the fluid as it makes its way down your oesophagus, in little liquid boluses. As it enters your stomach your shoulders involuntarily quiver.

You place a square of dark chocolate on your tongue, close your lips and sense it melt. You roll the chocolate around your tongue, let the flavonoids and other polyphenols enter your bloodstream through your soft palate. You revel in its warm sweetness, like a warm bath on a cold night. I join you in the cold snow and throw my own pack down.

Suddenly, your focus shifts from taste buds to a pin-point silhouette against the sky: a tiny figure on another mountain, high up on a ridge. Everything else – peaks, angular rock formations, the pencil line of the road down below – slides out of focus, becoming fuzzy, as though you are looking through a telescope, the mind's telescope. The telescope of perception.

Your journey thus far has been a journey of intense concentration and pleasure. You delighted in the delicacy of the mosses, and arriving here, in the snow, in this very moment, you have found that you have let go of your discomforts. You have loosened your grip on your anger. You are beginning to loosen your grip on your sadness. You didn't even know you were so sad. You've become proficient at sweeping grief up into a dusty pile in a recess of the mind. It's remained hidden, even to you. Just a gnawing doubt about you don't know what. Now it is time to let go of your anger. Let go of your grief. Let go of your sadness.

'I have been always preyed on by some dread,' Samuel Taylor Coleridge wrote in his *Notebooks*, 'and perhaps all my faulty actions have been the consequence of some Dread or other on my mind.' Coleridge would walk for forty miles at a stretch with William Wordsworth, although Thomas Carlyle, after meeting Coleridge, wrote that 'he does not tread, but shovel and slide. My father would call it "skluffing".' But Coleridge also knew that 'in nature there is nothing melancholy'.

This is how you just experienced The Mountain, right here on its very flanks, as an intricate pattern of internal and external sense perceptions. For Coleridge, simply going for a walk in wild nature can take us out of our current reality and deposit us in a kind of Nirvana, in another Garden of Eden. You are now aware of the meditative aspects of going for a walk on The Mountain. Of how, through treading mindfully in nature and seeing and feeling every detail of the landscape, our own bodies become a doorway. And what is more, how walking has a proclivity, if you do it often enough, for pushing us toward the edge of awakening.

8

PREPARATION

All things are ready, if our minds be so.

— William Shakespeare, *Henry V*, Act IV, Scene 3

You now prepare to climb.

You slip off your hiking shoes and socks. You squeeze each bare foot, in turn, into rock shoes that resemble ballet slippers. You lace them up slowly, making sure the laces threading through the second and fifth eyelets are slightly looser than the first and third, to give your toes and your arch more freedom. You do not need them so very tight, as you expect the climb to be well within your ability. You scrunch your toes three times to bed them in: neat as peas in a peapod.

You sit back against the rock face and reach for your harness. You squint up at the granite buttress that appears as a giant's headboard to the bed of the valley. Then you slip each leg carefully through the loops, taking care not to tangle them, and firmly buckle up the waist, feeding its tongue back on itself through the buckle for extra security. You click the plastic clasp of your chalk bag around your waist. The sound has a satisfying finality about it.

I uncoil the rope, dropping loop after loop carefully on the mat. You look up, your face warmed by the mid-morning sun, and read the rock face. A sacred text. The rock is caught by oblique light like an upturned beach at sunrise. The tide is low and each ripple diffracts the light as a lens would. The barrelled buttress disappears on both the left and the right. I pass you the end of a blue rope, your end, at the top of the pile, and it snakes through my fingers to yours. You look at me in silence and place the loose end on the mat. You won't tie in just yet.

You choose the hardware for the pitch. You decide on each nut and cam by judging the size of the placements in cracks discernible from the ground. This requires a level of knowledge about the cliff or the mountain that not everyone is party to. You realise how fortunate you are. An intricate crack stops and starts and varies between the diameter of a pencil and the thickness of a paperback. You study the crack until it eventually reaches its vanishing point.

You are re-familiarising yourself with your environment and learning more of this cliff. You have been here a handful of times before and can appreciate the importance of developing a sense of place. Knowing the landscape to such a depth that you know precisely what size a crack is on a remote cliff down to a millimetre is a very specific situation to be in. It's an important ritual you are undertaking here. The ritual of preparation.

You clip ten quick-draws to your gear loops with the karabiners' gates all facing out, so you can easily retrieve them from your harness, even in moments of extremis. You choose a double set of wires and six small to medium cams. There is no wide crack on the first pitch, so you can forget the big cams. You loop three slings bandolier-style across your chest. You twist your end of the rope into an exact '8', leaving plenty of tail to work with. You run the end up through your leg loops and then through your waist-belt and mindfully re-weave the '8'. You then squeeze the knot in your fist and pull the tail tight to complete the satisfying knar. Finally, you tie a single fisherman's knot to tidy up the lengthy tail.

All is done with the solemnity of a religious devotee. This is as any other ritual: a sacrament, giving thanks before a meal, making your bed in the morning. Reciting a mantra or turning the prayer wheel.

Om mani padme hum. All this is done to express the many dimensions of the human condition. Without even recognising it, for it is approaching the unfathomable, we are expressing an urgent need for purification from all this hatred and aggression. Our souls are crying out for a release from a possessiveness we can't seem to shake off. We are desperate to rid ourselves of all-devouring prejudice.

Equally, this ritual is performed, in all probability unbeknownst to each of us, as an aid in the realisation of the twin virtues of tolerance and generosity, and to assist us in gathering up those other strange bedfellows: perseverance and patience. In other words, to help us maintain the course of our moral compasses. To slowly acquire, by degree, wisdom. To achieve a state of grace. Though we are wholly unaware of all this, and simply think we are doing what we have always done below a cliff.

However, there are two kinds of ritual behaviours. The above are canon rituals: the canon of rock climbing. These include checking the weather forecast and avalanche conditions, inspecting your knot, glancing at your second's belay device, touching your helmet, boots and harness, to see all are snug.

All these are undertaken in the interest of safety, to lessen the risk of injury or death. Dirty boots will result in a slip of the foot and a plummet; choosing the wrong size protection will lead to long runouts and similarly dangerous outcomes. Just like the bottle placing and touching routine of Rafael Nadal before a serve, these rituals, however curious they may be, are success-driven. Nadal describes it as a way of ordering his surroundings, 'to match the order I seek in my head'. It is of ultimate importance in a game such as rock climbing to be thoroughly present; to be calm and place yourself in the zone of non-judgemental awareness required to succeed. To stay alive.

The other form of ritual is more difficult to get to unpack. This kind has meaning beyond its appearance. Before climbing in the Himalaya, mountaineers often hold a *puja*, a prayer ceremony where climbers place flowers, fruit and incense at the foot of the mountain or in a shrine. In Gangotri before attempting Meru Shark's Fin, Johnny Dawes, Philip Lloyd and I washed the lingam stone (a representation of Lord Shiva's penis) and garlanded it with orange flowers. In the Nepali village of Gokyo, we invoked the mountain gods to ask forgiveness for any damage we might do to the mountain, and to ask for the safety of the climbers.

Many mountaineers pray to all sorts of gods to keep them safe before they climb, but, as we have seen, rituals of the mountains do not have to be religious in nature. Another example of the non-religious type might be Eric Shipton smoking a pipe before he set off on his mountains. And before each expedition the legendary Polish mountaineer Wanda Rutkiewicz would receive a blessing from her mother in the form of a crucifix drawn on her forehead with her finger.

To mark out our intention is an important aspect of personal rituals. This prompts us to do our best, dispelling anxieties and subduing fears; to take back control by diminishing negative feelings and overcoming our tendency to procrastinate.

Ritual also moves us. We bracket important life events: marriages, deaths and births. We mark crucial transitions, like coming of age. Through ritual we can express ourselves in the joy of a life, and the sorrow of a death. But, most importantly, through our seemingly arcane rituals we fashion and perpetuate ourselves – our self. Our identity.

Humanity's forgotten ancestors created sacred rituals to firm the bonds of kinship that were essential to stay alive in a perilous world. Now, these bonds also signify allegiance to a particular group. Just as the Eucharist, the partaking of the body and the blood of Christ, signifies a profound connection to God, this ritual also signifies a connection to all Christians. In a similar way, having a craic with your mates at the base of the cliff – or, of course, the pub ritual at the end of a day's climbing – is not just about social cohesion but a vital connection to nature, to reality, to truth. To The Mountain.

Personal rituals can underline one's point, a pinprick of light among the great constellations of the universe. Engaging in these rituals means we are actively participating in our own lives. This return of personal responsibility allows us to be our best when we need to stay present in a harsh environment. When we need to act under pressure. Through this we create a sense of equilibrium in our lives. The ritual you follow at the base of the cliff proves *you* are responsible for how *you* live. You get to choose who you share your experience with on this grand voyage. You get to define yourself on this rocky promontory you inhabit.

There can be a touch of superstition in all this, but it works, so why not? Just as Dumbo can't fly without his white feather, and Jimmy Grimble can't play football without his magic boots, many climbers can't soar without a ritual talisman. Big-wall climber John Middendorf carried a Baja shark tooth as his lucky charm, all the way up *The Grand Voyage* on Great Trango Tower, a gigantic and difficult climb in Pakistan's Karakoram. Kevin Jorgeson wore a T-shirt designed by his dead friend every day on the famed *Dawn Wall* of El Capitan. And Lydia Bradey, the first woman to reach the summit of Mount Everest without supplementary oxygen, always takes a piece of turquoise to her summits.

When Celia Bull and I climbed the first ascent of *The Cornwall* on the North Tower of Paine in Patagonia, I had to leave my trusty MOAC nut on one of the rappel stations. This piece of protection was the first I'd bought aged sixteen, so it was a sad moment. I remember watching it disappear into swirling cloud as I descended the ropes. I had always carried it on my harness, never felt safe on a climb without it, and now it was gone. I bought another, but it wasn't the same. But that original MOAC *had* served its purpose and kept me safe.

At the foot of the climb you position a beer towel and stand on it. You bend down and put your fingers in the snow to wet them. You feel its refreshing coldness. You stand on one leg as if saluting the sun and rub the black sole of one rock slipper. You rub it vigorously, generating heat that evaporates any moisture. The hue of the sole changes from a dirty grey to a satisfying deep black. The other one now. Charcoal-black crumbs of rubber fall to the snow as you listen for the telltale squeak of a perfectly clean sole, which, like your very own starting gun, means you can begin.

You stand erect. Reaching out with your left hand, you touch the rock. This allows you to reacquaint yourself with its grainy texture; close up it has wavelets in the surface that remind you of the growth rings of a great tree. The rock is cold to the touch. Still, you have the feeling that you are about to climb on to the back of a great living beast.

You gently close your eyes. You reach around behind and whiten your hands with magnesium carbonate from the bag. You take a single deep breath, inhale and exhale, and open your eyes again. You rub your hands together to make sure they have an even coating of the chalk.

You are balanced on the liminal point, the threshold between not simply the horizontal and the vertical but between earth and heaven, outer and inner, between thought and reality, between mere exercise and transcendence, the frontier of life and death. You stand amazed, about to climb, poised between the ordinary and the extraordinary.

You give me a nod.

'I've got you,' I say.

'Climbing.'

9

THE CLIMB

... I stood on the peak in the strange thin air, looking into unimaginable distances. 'Yes,' I thought, 'this is it, my world, the real world, the secret, where there are no teachers, no schools, no unanswerable questions, where one can be without having to ask anything.' I kept carefully to the paths, for there were tremendous precipices all around. It was all very solemn, and I felt one had to be polite and silent up here, for one was in God's world. Here it was physically present.

— Carl Jung, *The Earth Has a Soul. The Nature Writings of C.G. Jung*

As your feet leave the safety of the little snow patch, your presence is demanded. You are forced to just be. Already risking a fall, you climb up on to the first step. I am holding your rope with all the concentration of a player absorbed in a game of chess. You are aware of this and draw comfort from it.

You look in front of your face and study the rock closely.

You focus your mind on a single hold. You study its texture. Is it grainy or smooth? Polished by years of traffic or with good gritty friction? What dimension is it? Pocket or edge? It is a pocket that will take two fingertips. But wait. There is an infinitesimally small depression for the tip of your index finger. That may be enough to take a couple more pounds of bodyweight.

Then your mind notices another option.

There is an edge the width of a matchbox up and right, just out of reach. You feel behind your back for your chalk bag, blow the excess off your fingers and choose the edge: you're always stronger on an edge. You adjust your feet, knowing instinctively this simple act will give you an extra inch for your right arm. You reach up and claw your index finger, your middle finger and your ring finger on to the edge. Once you know you have it securely, you bend your elbow five degrees and curl your thumb over the tips of your index and ring fingers.

All other thought has left your head.

Each of us has between 6,000 and 60,000 thoughts each day (depending on how you classify a thought): hideous thoughts, pleasant thoughts, negative thoughts, arousing thoughts, memories of ex-lovers, worries about unpaid tax bills and fears about paying the mortgage. These thoughts have to leave your head if you are to avoid injuring yourself, or worse.

I once reached a state of meditative absorption by painting a frozen waterfall blue with a yard brush, and I once met a woman who had a similar experience during a tennis match. But you can't die engaging in such artistic or sporting pursuits. Unless you are unlucky enough to get hit on the temple with a golf ball, that is.

Yet mountaineering and rock climbing are different, for there is an ever-present risk, however small, of death on The Mountain. And there's nothing like risking your neck to drag you kicking and screaming into the present. Of course, it is important to be able to feed your family and pay your tax bill. But with all these thousands of nagging thoughts running around your head, with this incessant chatter, you will not be able to focus your mind on one single issue.

And so, somewhere deep in your brain, you attend to the next task in hand, a micro adjustment of the heel of the thumb on your right hand.

The act of climbing a rock is extremely complex, but when you are in a state of flow your body movements are at a subconscious level. You do not think about where you are placing your feet while pacing down the pavement, and you aim to do the same climbing this rock: to move where the holds take you with ease, with flow.

With this inner game you are training your mind. The more you do this, the easier it becomes to focus your mind on everyday things. You are practising meditative absorption, or the one-pointedness of mind known in Sanskrit as *samādhi*. In *samādhi* the mind becomes still. It is a state of being completely aware of the present moment, a total immersion of the mind. 'The scattered mind is a weak mind,' S.N. Goenka once wrote. Though you do not have to struggle. All it takes is precise attention in every moment, to every move you make, what adherents of Vipassana meditation call *samma vayama* or 'right effort': mental effort.

What is more, 'right effort' can be continuous throughout our waking lives. We are meditatively aware in everything we do. A dedicated Vipassana practitioner would be meditating on eating, drinking, working and even going to the toilet.

In *samādhi* you are fully aware of your surroundings; your attention is drawn by the texture, hue, smell and feel of The Mountain. And back on the ground you are so aware that you begin to pre-empt the thoughts of people you meet, and recognise their individual moods in their faces. You are not simply a good judge of character but are approaching a heightened conscious state in these moments of awareness.

By developing our consciousness through climbing and being aware of our surroundings, we are training our minds to see the impermanent reality of being. And by doing so, we reach the conclusion that to be greedy, envious and cruel, or to generally act like a dick, works against us. As a consequence, we begin to lead a life where stealing, bad-mouthing and generally taking advantage of other people becomes unpalatable. This seems to be the basis of moral codes in all religion. From the Precepts in Buddhism to the Ten Commandments of the Old Testament, each has a similar set of guidelines to live by. 'Thou shalt not kill' and 'I undertake the training-precept to abstain from taking what is not given' are fairly good rules to live by. So, The Mountain Path, it appears, is circular, with mindfulness buttressing our ethical lives.

You realise this and are aware that one can't be in such a dangerous environment without being mindful, without engaging in some form of insight meditation. And the more you engage with The Mountain, you are training your mind, positively re-enforcing it. And you can feel the change already manifesting within yourself. After all, you have been actively engaging with the landscape every chance you get for the past few years.

You recognise that the present moment is happening when you misplace the point of your left foot.

You watch with a detached interest as the shoe leaves a black smudge of rubber on the wall. As it skids, there's a heartbeat's delay before you feel the stab of adrenaline in your chest. You are several body lengths above the last piece of protection. If you fall, you will smash yourself up. You make a conscious decision to be unafraid, and also not to beat yourself up about it, not to judge yourself. It works. You take strength from gaining control of the moment. You recognise this instance in time.

You hang on a great smooth hold, breathe, fiddle in an okay stopper and look down.

Take a long breath in. Rest. And in the long moment that follows you have this insight: 'Most people of a Buddhist persuasion believe enlightenment can only come from within and the search for ultimate reality must come from within also. Usually it is the breath that is the focus of concentration, as the breath is within you, a permanent fixture of your life. Sometimes it is the whole field of bodily awareness. But now you see clearly the breath is only as permanent as the rock on which you now climb. These lungs that voraciously suck oxygen into your body are just as liable to decay as the rock which forms this mighty cliff.'

You make out a slot above that may offer more protection. And so you climb two body-lengths higher without thought, without judgement.

You feel a great sense of space. The rope makes a neat zigzag pattern as it falls through the karabiners all the way into my hands. You touch the rock with the tips of your fingers. Its surface is warm and pulsing. In the harsh sunlight at this altitude you can feel the actinic process that breaks down the stone, minute layer after minute layer.

As your fingers creep into the slot, you notice you are already a long way above the scree field. You feel a great sense of space. And your body seems to be dissolving along with the rock face. Your body is becoming a space. Your whole being is becoming a space where the intention to move exists. Thoughts come. Thoughts go. You don't pay attention to them. You are aware they are distractions. As soon as they have left this space, you no longer recall what they were about. You are not forgetful. Nor are you uncaring. You are flowing like a stream of water.

You twist your right shoe into a crack.

There's a sudden pain in the big toe of your right foot. You feel yourself about to collapse back into your body. Then you quickly remind yourself that the pain is not of this moment. What you are experiencing as pain you have already dealt with. What you feel as pain is in fact the prospect of future pain in the next moment. By absorbing the pain in this moment, we learn equanimity. This simple fact, you realise, is the great liberator.

In many ways, all the moves of the climb can be seen as similar to a Brazilian *simpatia* or a Japanese tea ceremony. All segments of these ceremonies bring a devotee closer, by increment, to a universal truth. The practitioner may not even realise they are on a path, and she or he may never fulfil their true potential. But that is not the point. You know, don't you? Just to be on the path is enough. In a similar way the moves of a climb add together to convey the climber one step closer – and that step could be a great or small step – to seeing things as they really are. To experiencing reality as it actually is.

You hang on to the rock with one hand and gently touch its skin with the other. You close your eyes for three long seconds. Feel the pulse in your fingertips. Do you feel the rock vibrating? You let the rock merge with your body and feel the electrons and positrons orbiting the nuclei of every atom of the cliff. The same cosmic forces at work in your own body.

Now the left foot.

There are three choices: a good, paperback-spine-sized edge by your hip, a pocket into which a billiard ball would fit neatly by your left shin and a smear, ten degrees less in angle than the mean of the face, at thigh level. Which should you choose? The paperback spine is too near your body and will push you out of balance; the billiard pocket is too low. It will have to be the smear. So you use the billiard pocket as an intermediate foothold to give yourself a little more height and poise, then jump your left foot on to the smear. You momentarily recoil and through a mysterious sequence of elastic dynamics, like the spring of a grasshopper's leap, you gain a distant three-finger flat hold while your body is neither moving up past it or falling down and off the rock. A moment when you are weightless.

Any movement of the body is complex. The more we move our bodies in a measured and meditative way, the more mindful we become. We also become closer to ridding ourselves of the hindrances that constantly attempt to prise us off the rock and back into the world of trivia, of distraction, of things that don't serve us. Dragging us from a terrifying and beautiful reality.

Your mind is becoming confused through lack of oxygen. Breathe ...

You go inside your body and study what is happening. Your forearms are becoming hard, pumped with blood. Your breath is becoming laboured and you have to concentrate to ease it back. This is effective. Your proprioception tells you exactly where your body is on the rock, in time and in space. It also conveys to you each individual joint angle: left elbow ninety-five degrees, right leg eighty with the ankle at seventy. But, wait. You're also suddenly aware that your index finger is about to slip out of the small depression.

If you do not move in five seconds you will fall.

You breathe as the mountain breathes. You sweat as the mountain sweats. The mountain is alive as you are alive, its chill wind upon you. Seasons arrive. Seasons go. Stormy spring turns to fecund summer, from bare autumn to icy winter. The mountain stands tall and composed, rooted in the face of change. You have become The Mountain. Light and dark. Stillness and movement. Acceptance of all change. In this moment you can face anything with a calm resilience.

You feel the adductor brevis muscle stretch, become taut close to your groin as you strain to place your right foot on a high sloping edge.

And suddenly you are observing yourself as you climb. You feel a single grain of rock crush under your shoe like a grain of sugar. But is it you? You are not thinking consciously about the technicalities of the climb, not considering where to put your fingers or your toes. You are experiencing the climb from outside your body, mind, self. 'You are standing on the bridge watching yourself pass by,' as Ram Dass said.

You lock off your left arm so that your bicep almost touches your forearm. You then commence to rock over on to the high foothold. You reach up and aim your right hand towards a black hole in the smooth rock face. But your hand pulls up short. A miscalculation. You crane your left elbow so that it strains in extension just long enough for you to take the pocket. It swallows three fingers up to the second joint and you are able to relax for a moment. Your mind becomes quiet. You venture into that ocean of tranquillity and sink down into its calm. The sereneness of the mountain tarn you look down on.

In this moment you sense the ego wrenching itself out of your body. Is this what the soul is? Is this what happens when you die? The 'I' leaves the body? Is bodily death ego death?

It will come back.

All of a sudden you wake up. You are freed from all the unhinged dreams you confuse with reality. And in that instant, mistakenly perhaps, or because you aren't thinking enough to stop it from happening, like seeing a thing from the corner of your eye, you experience, in a flash, things as they really are. Just an inkling, but it's blinding. It's heaven, but not light and angels. Just the truth. Just the truth.

From climbing ever upwards, we learn to go inside, to meet the unexpurgated version of ourselves. Beware, though, often we do not like what we find there and attempt to keep it buried. We encounter what Buddhists know as The Five Hindrances: craving, ill will, torpor, anxiety and doubt. These Five Hindrances are real, but by focusing the mind on a single object repeatedly for months, years even, we find that the mind then does not wander so easily. By seeing things as they really are, it becomes easier to dispense with all this ill will, all this doubt, all this hate. Simply by moving the body we do away with torpor, and by developing equanimity through discomfort we learn that carrying the monkey mind of worry serves no purpose.

You stand up.

The only way to make progress in this unpredictable universe of ours is equanimity. Positive thinking is a hindrance. There can be no positive without a negative. We can't have positive thinking without negative thinking. You refrained from praising yourself when you just pulled off that clever dynamic move. And you did not castigate yourself when your shoe skidded off the rock. You are climbing with complete equanimity.

By doing away with all this judgement, you do not avoid seeing what to do in this moment. You do not add or take anything away from the arrangement of holds you experience. You observe the wall non-judgementally and with as much clarity as possible. The rock appears as it is, undistorted by verdict or opinion. Following this path, your mind remains calm.

You reach behind for some chalk to dry your fingers for the next move.

As you acquire the skills to keep yourself in complete equanimity, you decline to take those 'fear trips into the future'. You begin to rouse a previously dormant skill, which provides you with the essential resources to deal with whatever avalanches life sees fit to drop on your head. Even though things may be falling apart around you, if you are able to maintain this equanimity and balance, you will be of more benefit to yourself and others.

You edge a little higher.

In doing so you find freedom from what Buddhism calls The Three Poisons: greed, hatred and delusion. You realise that if we are easily seduced by possessions or people, we will find non-attachment up on the cliff. If we are haters, filled with negativity, only having bad words for people, we will find loving kindness up there. If we are deluded about our true natures, believing that we are indeed empty of self and there is no 'I', then we will find wisdom or at least non-bewilderment on The Mountain.

You climb into a depression.

It's essential to dislodge yourself from this inordinate attachment to your thoughts. You realise that if you are wrapped up in thought, then you are not really here, you are not really on this buttress of rock, so precariously balanced: you may as well be on that beach in Bali or back in the office. Of course, each of us has to do something ordinary with our lives. But, at this moment, you vow to bring this insight home. To work with care and concentration. To focus on what's right in front of you. To be present in each and every moment of your life.

You feel a shift in your consciousness. It's now hovering just above your shoulder. What you thought of as your 'self' – your consciousness – is moving further away. You look down at your frail body. It is you upon that immaculate curved shield of rock. And it is you doing the observing also. How can this be?

Then it happens.

There's a split in your fingertips. This you observe. Light begins to pour out from these splits. Barely a moment later, light begins to pour out of your mouth and then your nose, from all the orifices of your body, all the pores of your skin. You are made of light. In this moment you are incorporated into the universe: all the joy, and all the hardship, the yin and yang. You are among the planets, dissolved. Who you thought you were, all the labels – son, daughter, sister, brother, husband, wife, activist, partier, determined son-of-a-bitch – have utterly dissipated.

You are now pure consciousness. There is no space you can imagine that you are not already occupying.

You move swiftly, poetically, up the final slab, beyond the difficulties, beyond the hardship, beyond the suffering. You are literally bounding up the rock. No sooner have you caught a hold than you are past it and on to the next ledge or pocket. You are not searching the rock's features anymore and you are not worried about the lack of protection. Your body seems to instinctively know the language of the rock, the rock's music. Your body inhabits it. You can't conceal a grin. You are filled with joy.

As you flow towards the summit, you pause and look down. The whole world is below you.

'Am I in heaven?' you ask yourself.

It's the right question to ask. In this moment, you *are* in heaven, or at least at the *axis mundi*, where heaven meets earth, at the foot of a ladder to infinity. For you realise finally that heaven is on this fissured mountain. And it always has been.

Towards the top of the climb, you have a shift in perspective, though in reality you knew it all along. You are me; I am you. There is no 'I this' and 'I that'. There is only here, and now. That's all there is. And you become the postie down in the village below and you can feel his hand in the letterbox. You become the nibbling sheep, the lark ascending. You are not in the process of becoming one with the landscape. You are in a process of realisation that you always were one with the landscape. You are one with the world. You are the universe. You meld with The Mountain.

In this brief moment you see the only way out of here is through love and kindness and compassion. You see the way. Love yourself. Love the universe.

All about, there is utter silence, and in this silence you can see and hear all. Down in the valley, you watch grey mourners with inscriptions of sorrow on their faces lower an old miner into his grave. You listen carefully to the rattle of their breath, the phlegmy coughs, and wonder, without sadness, which of the others will follow next. In the shop, a young woman is arguing with an ex-partner on a mobile phone, something about a court case. Dogs bark. Out at sea, a whale blows. In the next village, the vicar is giving a young girl her first communion. 'This bread, which is broken for you, is my body.'

The air is chilly now on your bare arm.

You give thanks. Not with your voice, but you have a silent moment and take in the splendour of your surroundings. You take a deep breath and are content in a way you haven't been since you were last here. This is thanks enough.

You fetch me up on the rope.

On top of The Mountain, you allow yourself to come back into your body. You re-experience your body. However, a tiny piece of the climb stays with you on the descent. It will stay with you for the rest of this life. And when you go out to The Mountain next time, you will build on this consuming experience and find you will be able to access this transcendent state more easily. Hesse wrote, 'Every path leads homeward, every step is birth, every step is death, every grave is mother.'[1] You realise you can never get to the top. There is no summit. The top does not exist. But home does. And in order to get home, *you* must first die. Therefore, you surrender yourself to The Mountain Path.

We must return to the village now. The features of the mountain face, the nose, the cave mouth, the white fringe, absorb the slowly fading light. There is no trace of human passage, save for a darkening foot track that is shared with goats. The sun is setting now on the earth. The mountain tarn becomes a glowing, oily mirror. The shadows cast from the buildings are enveloping the fields.

You look to the sky and glimpse the burnished edge of a kestrel's wings. The solitary bird, with her wings outstretched, momentarily becomes a crucifixion. The light is blinding. You distil this final picture and turn.

You follow The Mountain Path back to the village.

---

1   *Trees: Reflections and Poems*, Hermann Hesse.

10

THE BOTTOMLESS CHASM

Who cannot bear the painful body-feelings that arise
endangering his life, he trembles when afflicted.
He wails and cries aloud, a weak and feeble man.
He cannot stand against the pit,
nor can a foothold he secure.
But one who bears the painful body-feelings that arise,
not trembling when his very life is threatened,
he truly can withstand that pit
and gain a foothold in its depth.

— Patala Sutta, from the *Samyutta Nikaya,*
translated by Nyanaponika Thera

Walking a path I have travelled many times before, I arrive at Cape
Hauy. To be on that cape, on that narrow rock promontory, is to
witness something as profound as anything in nature: the colourful,
lichened cliff dropping off into the barking Southern Ocean in un-
ironed pleats; the searchlight sun beaming down through holes in the
cloud cover, hunting for boats upon the dark surface of the sea;
a peregrine nest flecked with white, high up in one of the cliff face's

messy folds. There's a gull looking down at me as I stand on the edge of the world. I can't guess what it makes of this primeval scene: indifference, probably. Whereas this place and I? We have history. At this place I bled. At this place I was born into a new life.

One could be forgiven for overlooking something as unique in nature as the Totem Pole, even though it is part of the most extensive dolerite formation on Earth. We often overlook extraordinary things. Some understandably mistake it for the taller and thicker Candlestick, which, from this viewpoint, is indeed more impressive. The Candlestick is level with the cape and so close that David Warburton, school spitting champion when I was a boy, could, with a favourable wind, have gobbed on it.

If you turn your head to the right, the towering cliffs of Cape Pillar dominate the southern horizon. Beyond that is the Shackleton Ice Shelf. Columnar cliffs fringe the coastline to the north all the way to the distant Maria Island. And if you lean right out over the abyss and look down, you will see the Totem Pole's postage-stamp summit. It seems to be ploughing through the frothing sea corridor between you and the Candlestick. But it's only when you are level with the Totem Pole that you see just how unlikely it appears, being just four metres square and sixty-five metres tall. Some say it could topple over at any time, though I think it will still be standing a hundred years from now.

For the past eighteen years, on 13 February, I have made an annual pilgrimage to Cape Hauy. Or at least attempted the walk, weather and kids permitting. The first pilgrimage was my first anniversary. Still facing enormous difficulties in walking, I took a helicopter to within 500 metres of the lookout. Mid-February is still a very emotional time for me. I walk out to the cape for a number of reasons: in part to revisit the last walk I did as an able-bodied person, but also to put paid to any superstitious nonsense about Friday the thirteenth lingering in some squidgy recess of my reptilian brain. Mainly, though, it's because it's a fine hike in such grand surroundings.

Nevertheless, with each successive pilgrimage, I began to feel a hollowness creep into my mind when I arrived at the cape. A feeling of 'what now?' I would gaze down at the pole and feel something was missing. Slowly, as the years went by, a subconscious urge to climb the Totem Pole crept steadily forward from the back of my mind until it had become a burning ambition. Now I was back, peering over the recently installed and somewhat controversial barrier and feeling very different about this piece of rock. This time I had come to climb the thing.

Matthew Newton, or Newt as we called him, was going to film the whole event. We knew each other from several filming adventures, such as running Tasmania's remote Franklin River. Together with business partner Catherine Pettman, who was also at the cape, they make up Rummin Productions. Also included was my old friend John Middendorf, who carried his golf club out to the cape to practise his swing. There was head chef Andy Cianchi, Vonna Keller and Andy Kuylaars on safety, and acting as mules and moral support were Zoe Wilkinson, Margie Jenkin and Melinda Oogjes. I also had my attorney Jeffrey Blake in attendance, just in case. Altogether ten good friends and comrades with, last but not least in his capacity of rope gun, Steve Monks himself.

It is the Totem Pole that inextricably cements our relationship. Steve made the first free ascent in 1995 with Simon Mentz and Jane Wilkinson. Celia and I were headed for the second free ascent that Friday in 1998. Steve saw us off on our walk from Fortescue Bay. It was the first time that I had met him, but Celia and Steve knew each other well from times spent on the sea cliffs of south-west England.

The day after my accident, Steve was the one who made the Tyrolean traverse to the summit, abseiled down the Totem Pole, and cleaned it. Not literally scrubbing it clean, although he did say there was a lot of blood on it. There were 100 metres of rope and lots of equipment left there from the rescue effort. This included the frayed ends of the rope paramedic Neale Smith had needed to cut, with us hanging on it, to drop into the waiting rescue boat.

Exactly a year later I was the subject of a BBC film, *Wild Climbs: Tasmania*. My recovery was cut with footage of Steve and his partner Enga Lokey climbing the Totem Pole. The film was why the Tasmanian National Park Service had given us special dispensation to fly within 500 metres of the end of the cape. I was too ill at that stage in my recovery to walk the six kilometres of rough track to Cape Hauy. The crew recorded my at times maudlin thoughts as I looked down at my friends performing the sort of gymnastic feats I had been capable of doing until exactly a year before.

When I first mooted the idea of climbing the Totem Pole again, there was no other partner I even considered. It had to be Steve. Luckily, he was all over it like a rash and began making preparations for the ascent. Even though he is an Englishman, Steve spends half his time in Natimuk, Victoria to be near 'the best crag in the world', Mount Arapiles. So, it was only a hop, skip and a jump for him to come over from the big island. As the appointed hour approached, we had several phone conversations about techniques, ropes and gear and how we would approach the climb.

The weekend arrived, and for me a difficult trek to the lookout. I took my first fall only a hundred metres from the car park, tripping under the weight of my backpack in front of a woman walking wearily towards me at the end of her five days on the Three Capes Track. I grazed my hand on the gravel path and in my embarrassment refused the helping hand of Melinda, who was walking just ahead of me. After brushing myself off I thought it best to ignore this hiccup and start again. I fell once more going up a flight of huge steps that could only have been made for giants. This time, in my fatigued state, my right foot failed to clear the step and I went down in a clatter of walking poles and callipers. Melinda and I sat on the steps for a while until Steve came back to see what the matter was. Even though he was already carrying a massive backpack, he took my bag and deposited it at the top of the hill. The walk to the end of the cape went more easily from that point on.

Melinda and I dropped our bags and I stumbled directly over to the guardrail. The previous day's wild weather with its four-metre swell had fallen, but only by a metre or so. It was still rough as guts down in the depths of the chasm. At the base of the pole, foaming waves were surging in from two directions and colliding in a plume of froth. I had little faith that we were going to be able to cross that soaking gap in the morning.

Andy got a brew on and passed around slices of his Antarctic fruit cake (Andy works in Antarctica) that was more marzipan and icing than cake. As the sun sank, a very cute native rat scurried from bush to backpack, while Newt tried unsuccessfully to capture it on film. We unfurled our sleeping mats and bags on the hard rock platform at the very edge of the cape. I unpeeled the Velcro straps on my calliper with an audible rip and wriggled down into my sleeping bag while Melinda read a few pages from Pema Chödrön's *The Places That Scare You*. We talked a bit about Chödrön's path of the warrior and how he or she accepts that we can never know what will happen to us next:

We can try to control the uncontrollable by looking for security and predictability, always hoping to be comfortable and safe. But the truth is that we can never avoid uncertainty. This not knowing is part of the adventure, and it's also what makes us afraid.

Melinda's mindful leanings mean she is brave, but she's not a climber, and these things are what drew me to her. We were both very busy being part-time single parents, deeply immersed in bringing up our children to be sensitive human beings. Besides, nowadays, I have little time for going climbing, preferring to read a book or go on walks or cycle expeditions. She is an artist working for people with disabilities, so understands when she sends me out to the shop to buy bread and milk and I come back with bananas and mangoes.

This was Melinda's first night sleeping under the stars for a decade and we awoke at the same time in the early hours of the morning. The night sky was ablaze with stars. The diamantine path of the Orion Arm arced the full breadth of burning space from the west horizon to the east. We sat up stargazing and whispering to one another for an hour and then snuggled back into our warm down bags.

On peeking out at the dawn, I was greeted by the lens of Newt's camera in front of my face. There was not a breath of wind, and peering over the edge of the cliff I could see the wild seas had abated. The churning tide had turned from white foam to green, gently lapping waves. I must admit to feeling a little nervous. No more was I a free-and-easy twenty-something (or even thirty-something). I had my children to think about. How would they be provided for if anything happened to me? Gobbling anticonvulsants, I worried also about having another fit, as I had the previous November in the Point To Pinnacle race. That time I had ended up in hospital with a six-month driving ban. Yet these feelings were only fleeting. All my hard work with acceptance now meant I could see the situation for what it was. The thousands of times on a cliff or mountain that I had recognised my fear and then climbed anyway were now paying off. And besides, I was in the safest of hands with Steve and the rest of the team.

After porridge and buckets of sweet tea, I sought out a quiet spot on the cliff edge to practise my morning meditations, basically some quiet time to reflect and summon up some inner strength. And then it was time to set off on our descent. A narrow climber's path takes you halfway down the cliff, and at times we had to clamber down three-metre rock steps. I was connected to Steve by a short rope, a sort of umbilical cord, to catch me if I should slip. There were times when this lifeline was essential, as the boot-wide path traversed the very edge of the precipice.

When we arrived at twin bolts sunk into the rock, I was struck by how unfamiliar my surroundings were. It was as if I was seeing the oh-so-close summit of the Totem Pole and peering over the edge of the cliff into the chasm below for the very first time. Forming memories is not as simple as it would first appear. In the brain, short-term or working memory makes its way from the prefrontal lobe down neural pathways to the hippocampus. If the memory is worth keeping, as opposed to a phone number you use once or a planned move you thought about but didn't actually make in a chess game, say, it becomes what is known as an episodic memory.

This place, of all places, ought to have been included in a vast treasure-house of episodic memories but it wasn't, thanks to my accident. It takes about two weeks for an episodic memory to be embedded in the various necessary areas of the cortex. Depending on the severity of a Traumatic Brain Injury (TBI) and, presumably, the area of one's head that took the knock, short-term memory doesn't have the opportunity to become embedded as it would normally. So, I was effectively seeing the Totem Pole from this angle for the very first time.

As I watched Steve disappear into the void, I was engulfed by a serene calm. I had made it. I was here. I looked up at the team of people helping me. We were all here.

A shout from below.

'Come on down!'

I took care fixing my abseil device on to the rope and slid over the edge. Once in the vertical world I felt at home again. Breathing a sigh of relief, I knew the climb was now underway and I could concentrate on the job in hand. I was once again living in the moment, and in this actual moment I was rappelling down to climb the Totem Pole.

For the past five years, I had been thinking with increasing frequency about going back to climb this needle of rock for a second time. And there had not been a day since the accident eighteen years earlier when I hadn't thought about the Totem Pole. In fact, each morning when I got out of bed and nearly fell over, there it was again, casting its shadow over me like a sundial. Yet I haven't been consumed or obsessed by this dolerite pillar. It has *not* been my Moby Dick. I have *not* been a Captain Ahab chasing my white whale. It is just that every single time I can't achieve something, every time I face an added challenge in my life, such as tying my shoelace or buttoning my shirt, driving my 'ute' (my pick-up truck) with only my left foot, or swimming (I have a crazy one-armed backstroke style), it's the Totem Pole

I have to thank. And thank it I must. For all this hardship does condition the mind.

I arrived at a ledge just above the tideline. It was damp with spray and the kelp was lifting with each surge of water through the narrow gap. Steve was tied to two bolts at the base of the Totem Pole, just above the sea. We could almost touch our outstretched hands, as in Michelangelo's *The Creation of Adam*. There was a thin piece of taut cord left by Canadian Sonnie Trotter, who had made a groundbreaking, one-pitch free ascent a few days before Steve and I arrived. This I used to pull myself across on to the pinnacle and then clipped my tether into the bolts. Only then did I allow myself to gaze up at the Totem Pole's immensity.

Life, for me, has always been about facing fears head-on and here I was, again, at the base of this great Ashokan pillar. I hung on the belay and stroked the marks in the rock, trying to make sense of the Totem Pole's inscribed edicts. Steve set off climbing. The rope bag hung between my legs and I had to be careful not to pull him off when he suddenly pulled the rope up to make a clip. The belay device, called a GriGri, worked well for my one-handed belaying technique under normal earth-bound conditions. Yet here, hanging above the sea, the rope got stuck repeatedly. Luckily, Steve is one of the most patient people I have ever met. And though he would not care to admit it, he is a shining example of one who has learnt much through his long journey in the mountains.

Meanwhile, I was hanging just a couple of metres from the place where I once hung upside-down with my brains spilling out into the sea. I searched for more reasons why I felt compelled to attempt such a, some would say – and indeed have said – insane feat. Not the least reason was my need to close an eighteen-year linear line into a loop. Isn't that what everybody wants to do? Come full circle? Not to return to how things were in the beginning – that's not what I mean and would be impossible for me now. But to travel from the glorious optimism of youth, to pain and, for me, not an insignificant amount of pessimism, and then back to glorious optimism again, yet, with more positivity than before – for me there was no other course of action.

About a year after my accident, I made a conscious decision to begin living life with renewed vigour. In *Middlemarch* George Eliot wrote, 'Every limit is a beginning as well as an ending.' Just as in Buddhism, death precipitates birth. Coming within a hair's breadth of death seemed to promote an attitude of living my life to the full at every opportunity. Not living my life at a million miles an hour, but simply trying to be present for every single moment of it.

So, for me, life is not a closed loop; it is a spiral, forever gaining height. With each hurt, forever gaining experience and knowledge. With each outing to the wild places, becoming freer. With each slice of solitude, grace. And with each new contact, trust. Becoming more at peace with myself, as if life were a rope, forever snaking around and up a great rock pillar.

For years I could not conceive of the difficulties surrounding climbing the Totem Pole. Not the least of my concerns were the technicalities of the ascent. Until very recently, I had considered climbing a rope with one arm and one leg impossible, for me at any rate. I knew of a number of climbers with paraplegia who had ascended El Capitan, that thousand-metre shield of rock in California's Yosemite Valley. However, a paraplegic has two working arms, and a T-bar rope ascender effectively turns the rope-climbing clamp, or jumar, into a pull-up bar. Of course, this requires a Herculean effort, but it is much more complicated to climb a rope with one arm and one foot, not least for being constantly off balance.

There was also the small fact that it was nigh-on twenty years since I had done a one-arm pull-up. I used to do it with a flick of my body, trickery really, but now my spastic right side would not allow me the flexibility needed for this flick. What's more, in my twenties I weighed fifty-seven kilos; now, twenty years later, I weighed sixty-eight. So I was convinced that climbing sixty metres of rope with only the left half of my body was out of the question. That's part of the reason

I had kept pushing the idea to a pitch-dark corner of my mind.

However, as some ideas do, this one became increasingly hard to keep in that dark corner and eventually it found its way to the middle of my room.

Big wall climbing legend John 'Deucey' Middendorf lives just across the River Derwent from me in Tasmania. He's an old friend from the States. Deucey had a colleague staying over, British big-wall climber Chris Trull. Chris had just climbed the Totem Pole days before the three of us met in John's garden.

'What if I could climb the Totem Pole after all these years?' I said to them. 'What if I could work it out somehow?'

John and Chris were convinced that it was possible, that they could design a system for me whereby I could, with my one useable leg and one useable arm, get some mechanical advantage. Together they worked out a two-to-one pulley system on jumars, which effectively halved my bodyweight. This we tested on John's static trapeze in his garden. It felt very easy to move my weight, but clunky and complicated with a mess of rope in front of my face. Added to this, for each pull-up I completed, I only seemed to gain ten centimetres in height on the rope. I needed a different, simpler system.

Another good friend, sailmaker David Ross, introduced me to the one-to-one system he used for climbing yacht masts. He hung a rope off the balcony above his workshop and I, like Romeo (or perhaps Quasimodo), ascended, accompanied by much grunting, to the portico. This system was much simpler than the two-to-one, but required much more effort as I was pulling my whole bodyweight. My diminutive American climbing partner Vonna Keller and I took the new system to a local cliff for a real test. Vonna led up the gently overhanging cliff with style and tied the rope to the bolts at the top of the sandstone wall. I then jumared up the rope, quite quickly I thought, with forty-odd one-arm pull-ups. I now knew I had a system that was going to work, and all that remained was to polish it. The Totem Pole is broken into two sections, or pitches, by a comfortable ledge (I should know, I lay there for seven hours). This sofa-sized ledge is not quite halfway. So I knew I only had to climb thirty metres in one push before getting a long rest.

It was from this ledge that Steve was now calling down, 'Safe, Paul!' Then he pulled up the slack in the rope while I struggled to keep it untangled as it rose out of the bag like a knotty charmed snake. When the ropes were taut to my harness I realised we had a problem. Our two ropes had become mixed up with the cord the Canadians had left. I had tied my knots to my harness so tightly that I couldn't undo them with one hand very easily. I was effectively trapped. I was just about to call up for a knife when, as if by magic, one arrived right in front of my nose. Steve had been keeping an eye on me and, noticing my problem, had clipped the knife to the slack he'd pulled in and slid it down. I had only to touch the cord lightly with the sharp blade and it sprang apart.

I was about to unclip myself from the belay when what sounded like bomb explosions began reverberating through the narrow cleft. Looking up, I couldn't make out where the missiles were coming from, but I could guess. Someone was throwing rocks over the railing of the lookout about 120 metres above our heads. The rocks were hitting the water not far from where I was hanging. Vonna, who was taking still photographs, scrambled with extreme haste up to the lookout while we all screamed, 'Hey, there's people down here!' I doubt they heard our violent protestations over the deafening sea.

When Vonna arrived at the lookout she found it deserted, so she began running up the track in the direction of the car park. It was one aggravated Midwestern farmer's daughter who eventually confronted two hikers on the path. They admitted to tossing rocks over the lookout to hear the echoing splash.

'You could have murdered someone down there! Do you realise that?'

Vonna may be diminutive, but she is one of the most capable and resilient people I have ever met, and I wouldn't like to be on the wrong side of her.

'You should know better at your age!'

After reducing one of the stone throwers to tears and extracting profuse apologies from them, she turned around and came back down the steep descent.

After extricating myself from the belay, I made the exact same swing that I had made over eighteen years before, the swing that had dislodged the rock and left me hanging upside down, blood pouring from my head into the sea. A shiver went the length of my spine. Attempting to force my neck down into my torso, I waited anxiously for the fatal blow. It did not come.

When my swing came to a halt, I was so close to the seething kelp that my climbing shoes were getting wet. So I set off up the wall, making long one-arm pulls, trying to get some distance between my feet and the waves. Sliding the clamp up as far as I could reach above my head, I tucked my frame into the rope and stood up. It was strenuous but I knew I could do it, even if I couldn't always manage it. My spastic right leg was kicking the rock with some force and hurting my big toe as I unclipped each piece of protection that Steve had put in for his safety.

Despite that, all was going well. I was climbing my rope up the face. And then it was as if a child was messing about with the tuning knob on an old TV. Static, white noise, then I am back to my last time, eighteen years earlier, being laboriously hauled up in six-inch jerks, a limp rag of my former self. It was a flash of images. Then more static. Then back on the wall with Steve peering over the edge of the ledge. The crackle of white noise again and Steve's face becomes Celia's for a fraction of a second. I was becoming disoriented and had to pull myself together.

And then I was there, at the rock scar, the hole where the block came from that changed everything. I gasped involuntarily. I knew the rock that hit me was big, but this was a huge, axe-shaped scar, about the size of a laptop. Perhaps it had broken up as it fell the twenty-five metres on to my head, of perhaps more had fallen out in the intervening eighteen years. It was impossible to say.

I caressed the rock scar and tears welled up in my eyes. I was not sad or angry. I had accepted what had happened a long time ago. So why was I crying? It dawned on me then that I had waited almost two decades to come back to this place, to return to this stack in the sea that had given me so much. Touching, stroking that scar, an image of Celia flashed through my mind – not a picture, just a feeling. Then Neale Smith, who had rescued me. Then Glenn Robbins, who had pulled me from the water below Gogarth. Then Nick Kekus, who had lowered me down that gully when I fell in Scotland. Then my mother. All the people I owed my life to. And the others, unknown to me, to us, who inadvertently save our lives every day.

The whole of this trip, the walk-in, the friends, the Milky Way last night shared with Melinda, the descent shared umbilically with Steve, all these recent memories were flashing in and out of my mind alongside the old ones. I felt a pure and simple gratitude for this moment. For being alive. At that moment I was overwhelmed by life. It was as though my whole eighteen-year Totem Pole journey slid neatly into this laptop-shaped slot in a crack just below the ledge. My life with all its twists and turns, everyone's lives with all their twists and turns. I suddenly felt a deep connection to everyone. I WAS ALIVE! And that was enough, for now at any rate.

I was now at the right-angled edge of the ledge and needed to clamber on to it, like climbing on to a tabletop. This was the hardest part for me in 1998. Celia's voice suddenly rang in my head:

'You're going to have to help me here if we're to get you out of this.'

It was as if it were yesterday. I could hear the timbre of her voice, not calm but certainly not panicking. I could still hear her intense gasps as she woman-hauled me on to that ledge. I recalled how in my attempts to help her to help me I first became aware that my right arm and leg were not functioning at all. Reaching that ledge had been the finish for me that day, but now we still had work to do and thirty-five metres to climb. I could not lose myself for long to these ghosts.

When I had clambered on to the ledge, Steve tied me to the belay bolts and then noticed something was missing.

'Where's the cheat stick, then?'

Steve had an extendable painter's pole that he called his 'cheat stick'. He would use it if the ground between the bolts was too difficult to climb, allowing him to clip bolts that would otherwise be out of reach. Unluckily for him, Steve's cheat stick had been unclipped with the mêlée of tangled rope just above the sea, and ended up in the drink.

'I lost it,' I said, without trying too hard to conceal a grin. Losing the cheat stick meant he would be forced to climb free all the way up the pole. 'There will be no cheating on the Totem Pole,' I added. 'Not on my ascent.'

We both laughed heartily.

Steve told me that subsequent to my accident, when he was down here cleaning up the rope and gear, the ledge had been covered in blood. I remember him returning a blood-soaked scarf, which I kept for a few years but thought it best to leave behind in Wales when I moved to Australia. After a slug of water, and a squeak of the rubber soles on his climbing shoes, he set off on the top pitch, climbing with a grace that belied his years. As I write this, he's in his fifties, yet Steve still climbs with all the athletic elegance of a thirty-year-old. He didn't need his 'cheat stick'. I had a much easier time belaying one-handed as I wasn't hanging above the water with the rope bag dangling between my legs. The ropes were laid out, neatly coiled on the ledge and fed through the GriGri with ease.

Much as I tried, I could not stop scrutinising my immediate surroundings, the ledge where I had so nearly died. There was a negative of me – no, an imprint – there. Lying on the ledge. I rested my cheek on the warm grey rock and re-familiarised myself with its granular texture. I recalled the mixture of blood and cerebrospinal fluid that was steadily leaking out from under the helmet Celia had placed on me – like spilt gravy pooling on a tabletop. I felt the pain as

Neale Smith fitted a hard collar to stabilise my neck. I felt him now, lifting me like a ragdoll to clip my harness to his harness. I felt myself being dragged to the edge to drop back down the wall that Celia had so courageously hauled me up all those hours ago.

Celia was weighing heavily on my mind. How must she have felt, jumaring up the pole, leaving that pile of bloodied rags behind on the ledge? Had she glanced down at any time to see me slowly expiring in the recovery position? Was she shaking on the summit? I imagined her fumbling the karabiner as she attempted to clip it on to the rope traverse, dragging herself across, the swimming void below her. How must she have felt? Did she look back at the ledge while scrambling up to the lookout? How did she cope, running on the track past tourists to the car park? How does she feel now? We talk often, but not about such things. I can't even begin to guess. A wave, not liquid but a deep sound wave of sorrow, resonated through me. I looked up, still keeping half an eye on Steve, no matter how deep my reverie wanted to take me.

Steve was almost at the summit now and had made the climb appear easy, only seeming to struggle once, at the end of a run-out section. He began slapping the eastern edge of the Totem Pole with an increasing haste that was almost imperceptible. I only noticed the slight panic in his sudden movements as they were transmitted down the rope. I took in a few inches of slack and shouted encouragement. Then he was back to his calm, pacific self. That was the extent of it. And then he was on top.

'Safe!' came a call from above. Then, a couple of minutes later, 'Come on up!'

Fixing my ascenders to the thin line, I unclipped from the belay bolts. When weighted, dynamic lead rope stretches, so I ended up sagging back on to the ledge. Then I began, in my struggle to climb the rope resembling a sort of absurd marionette, crazily dancing up and down on a little stage. That made Steve the puppeteer, controlling me from above. Eventually, leaving the safety of the ledge, I began to make steady progress up the vertical wall.

About halfway up the top pitch, I heard from below a distinctive honking, like the Indian conch-shell horn I gave my son Eli for his birthday. Looking down, I saw a seal on a sea-washed ledge. When the seal barked, I barked. When I barked, the seal barked. We were talking to each other – the only difference being that the seal knew what it was saying.

I slid my top clamp up the rope as far as it would go.

I leant forwards against the rope.

With my left heel touching my left buttock, I struggled to stand up.

As I rose, the ascender on my chest harness slid up the rope automatically. As it did so, it made a comforting zip-like noise, comforting because I knew ground gained was ground won. You can't slip backwards on these clamps. I stood until my leg was pin-straight.

'Ninety-three,' I said to myself. I was counting my moves, my one-arm pulls up the rope.

At each bolt I would pause. Unclip rope from karabiner … Unclip karabiner from bolt … Clip karabiner to harness … This rhythm would normally have been a meditation, but perhaps there were too many eyes on us, including the eye in the sky, the buzzing drone there to get the aerial footage.

As I climbed higher, the Totem Pole itself seemed to disappear at sea level to the width of the rope on which I was now dangling. It was a crazy trick of perspective. Freezing stock still, I tried to sense whether the pole was swaying. A friend of mine had once said he felt it swaying in the wind when he stood on the summit. It was some consolation that I couldn't feel any movement. Though this was only a gentle breeze.

'One hundred and ten.'

Almost there now. The pain in my left shoulder was worsening. With all the pulling, I was having to shake the lactic acid out of my arm every four moves.

'One hundred and sixteen.'

I counted on the outbreath. Jumar up. Straighten leg. Then came the crux of the whole climb: a one-metre roof that my right leg automatically found and got stuck under. It took me at least ten minutes to negotiate this overhang.

'One hundred and nineteen.'

Seven moves later, my one hundred and twenty-sixth pull-up saw my torso rise above the level of the summit. My legs, however, remained below it. It appeared that I was stuck, and nothing Steve did seemed to help. For another ten minutes, I struggled to get on to the top, enmeshed as I was in knots and hardware. Eventually, I heaved my right leg with my left hand and positioned it on the absolute corner of the summit block. But now it was as if I was fixed to the spot, like an upright Gulliver unable to move in the tangle of Lilliputian ropes. I soon knew what I had to do, however; there was only one course of action.

I simply allowed myself to fall on to the summit, landing on Steve's bare feet, my legs sticking out over the abyss. I had made it. I had completed my eighteen-year climb to the summit of the Totem Pole. And here I was on top, kissing my dear leader's foot.

I complained about the smell. I laughed. We both laughed.

He put out his hand and helped me to a standing position, but I was barely stable, so fatigued and spastic were my legs. So after a hug I thought it best to sit down and conduct operations from a cross-legged posture.

Steve zipped himself across the Tyrolean and I was left alone on that fragile tower of dolerite. I crossed my legs, closed my eyes and let my mind drift. Why had I felt the need to climb this, the Totem Pole, of all things? The rock spire that on the face of it had caused me so much misery. Was it to prove myself amongst my peers? Was it to prove something to myself? That I was still a capable man? That I was still strong, even though I was disabled?

No. To me it was obvious, although so obvious that I found it virtually impossible to explain the reasons to myself, let alone anyone else. A host of confused motives seemed to manifest themselves to me as I sat there. And a simple feeling of extreme wellbeing flooded over me. The reasons to climb are the same as any human endeavour. Why do we do anything? My life had led me to this moment. I knew that. But what else?

I knew I wanted to give a message to other disabled people that to be disabled does not mean to be unable. What is more, to people struggling more generally in life, that it is possible to climb out of the morass that we find ourselves in too often.

What did it mean? Sitting on my own atop this rock needle, I saw, again, there is no personal, no us and them, no foreign and familiar, no feminine and masculine; we do not cast a shadow or have a reflection; there is no light or dark. All these dualities are merely two sides of the same whole. We are simply one.

On a personal level, my eighteen-year journey was the journey back to myself. I still have my old wobbles of insecurity from time to time. The familiar black dog comes still, rushing from the recesses of my mind. 'Don't you go letting life slip away without grabbing it by the balls.' I think we all suffer from these types of feeling at one time or another. So yes, climbing the Totem Pole is yet another attempt to squeeze a little more out of life. I am also aware of how futile this is and how it sets us up for suffering in the long term. And my climb was so much more than a wringing-out of life's sponge.

Then, all the motives and reasons seemed to coalesce, like rolling a snowball down a hill. In climbing the Totem Pole, I fully engaged, once again, with a challenge that has questioning at its heart. This curiosity about life is what wills me to keep going back to the wild places, and I will keep plumbing the depths of what these experiences can teach me for as long as I am able. Now, I realise all I have to do is show some bravery, even if underneath I am actually terrified. And in the process of repeatedly being courageous, I become true to myself. Climbing, striving and undergoing painful experiences is all part of a process, an ongoing lesson in trust, fear, dedication and challenge.

I do not even begin to pretend to have all the answers. But, one thing I am sure of: when we go to The Mountain, the great cliffs, with our minds fully open, we are one step closer to experiencing reality as it actually is. One step closer to the truth of the universe. And one step closer to transcendence.

As long as I am moving forward on the path, skyward on the mountain path, I am content. I am content to be on this road always, to not ever arrive. And this is of great consolation. Though, sometimes, especially at night, I do still ask the darkness one question.

'What the hell am I doing here?'

FURTHER READING

Abbey, Edward (1971), *Desert Solitaire: A Season in the Wilderness*, New York: Ballantine Books.

Aeschylus (*c.*458 BC), translated by Philip de May (2003), *Agamemnon*, Cambridge: Cambridge University Press.

Ariès, Philippe, translated by Patricia M. Ranum (1975), *Western Attitudes Toward Death: From the Middle Ages to the Present*, Baltimore: Johns Hopkins University Press.

Atisha (eleventh century), translated and edited by Ruth Sonam with commentary by Geshe Sonam Rinchen (1997), *Atisha's Lamp for the Path to Enlightenment*, New York: Snow Lion.

Becker, Ernest (1997), *The Denial of Death*, New York: Free Press.

Chalmers, David J. (1996), *The Conscious Mind*, New York: Oxford University Press.

Chödrön, Pema (2005), *The Places That Scare You*, Boulder: Shambala.

Chödrön, Pema (2006), *When Things Fall Apart*, Boulder: Shambala.

Coffey, Maria (2008), *Explorers of the Infinite*, New York: Penguin.

Coleridge, Samuel Taylor, edited by Earl Leslie Griggs (1956), *The Collected Letters of Samuel Taylor Coleridge, Volume 2: 1801–1806*, Oxford: Oxford University Press.

Dass, Ram (1978), *Be Here Now*, Santa Fe: Hanuman Foundation.

Daumal, René (1952), *Mount Analogue: A Novel of Symbolically Authentic Non-Euclidean Adventures in Mountain Climbing*, translated by Roger Shatuck (1971), San Francisco: City Lights Books.

Erdman, David V. (editor) (1988), *The Complete Poetry and Prose of William Blake*, New York: Anchor Books.

Evans-Wentz, W.Y. (2000), *The Tibetan Book of The Dead*, Oxford: Oxford University Press.

Feldenkrais, Moshe (1991), *Awareness Through Movement*, Middlesex: Penguin.

Feynman, Richard P.; Robert B., Leighton; Matthew Sands (1965), *The Feynman Lectures on Physics, Volume 3*, Boston: Addison-Wesley.

Gandhi, M.K. (1955), *Truth Is God*, Ahmedabad: Navajivan Trust.

Garfield, Jay L. (translator) (1997), *The Fundamental Wisdom of the Middle Way: Nagarjuna's Mūlamadhyamakakārikā*, Oxford: Oxford University Press.

Hanh, Thich Nhat (2015), *How to Walk*, Berkeley: Parallax.

Hart, William (2009), *The Art of Living: Vipassana Meditation: As Taught by S. N. Goenka*, San Francisco: HarperOne.

Hesse, Hermann (1972), *Wandering: Notes and Sketches*, New York: Farrar, Straus & Giroux.

Jung, Carl (2002), *The Earth Has a Soul: C.G. Jung on Nature, Technology & Modern Life*, Berkeley: North Atlantic Books.

Koch, Christof (2019), *The Feeling of Life Itself: Why Consciousness Is Widespread but Can't Be Computed*, Cambridge, Massachusetts: MIT Press.

Macfarlane, Robert (2003), *Mountains of the Mind: A History of Fascination*, Cambridge: Granta.

Macfarlane, Robert (2018), *The Old Ways: A Journey on Foot*, Cambridge: Granta.

Martin Heidegger (2010), *Being and Time*, translated by Joan Stambaugh, Albany, New York: SUNY Press.

Maslow, Abraham (1964), *Religions, Values, and Peak-Experiences*, New York: Penguin.

Nietzsche, Friedrich, translated by R.J. Hollingdale (2003), *Beyond Good and Evil*, Middlesex: Penguin.

Nuland, Sherwin B. (1995), *How We Die*, New York: Vintage.

Osho (2013), *The Art of Living and Dying*, London: Watkins Publishing.

Powers, John (2008), *A Concise Introduction to Tibetan Buddhism*, New York: Snow Lion.

Radhakrishnan, S. (translator) (1971), *Bhagavadgītā*, London: George Allen & Unwin.

Rank, Otto (2004), *The Myth of the Birth of the Hero*, Baltimore: Johns Hopkins University Press.

Ricard, Matthieu and Trinh Xuan Thuan (2004), *The Quantum and the Lotus: A Journey to the Frontiers Where Science and Buddhism Meet*, New York: Crown.

Sagan, Carl (1980), *Cosmos*, New York: Random House.

Santideva (seventh century), translated by Vesna A. Wallace and B. Alan Wallace (1997), *A Guide to the Bodhisattva Way of Life*, New York: Snow Lion.

Schaik, Sam van (2011), *Tibet: A History*, New Haven: Yale University Books.

Schmid, Stephen E. (editor) (2010), *Climbing: Philosophy for Everyone*, Chichester: Wiley-Blackwell.

Schopenhauer, Arthur (first published 1850), *On The Suffering of the World*, translated by R.J. Hollingdale (2005), London: Penguin.

Schwartz, Barry (2003), *The Paradox of Choice: Why More is Less*, New York: Ecco.

Tapovan, Sri Swami (2015), *Wanderings in the Himalayas*, Mumbai: Chinmaya Mission.

Thera, Nyanaponika (editor) (1997), *The Heart Sutra, Samyutta Nikaya*, Ukiah: Buddhist Text Translation Society.

Thoreau, Henry David (2018, first published 1862), *In Praise of Walking*, Bedford, Texas: Franklin Classics.

Tolle, Eckhart (2005), *A New Earth*, London: Penguin.

Tononi, Giulio (2012), *Phi: A Voyage from the Brain to the Soul*, New York: Pantheon.

Wolpe, Joseph and David Wolpe (1981), *Our Useless Fears*, Boston: Houghton Mifflin Company.

Yalom, Irvin D. (1980), *Existential Psychotherapy*, New York: Basic Books.

ACKNOWLEDGEMENTS

Writing what essentially amounts to a philosophy book had its difficulties for me, for I am no Naess or Nietzsche. Nevertheless, because of the experiences I have had on the cliffs and mountains, I do feel I have something to say. I am not formally schooled in philosophy, with the possible exception of the Buddhist kind. Consequently, I disappeared down paths of research for whole weeks, often coming up with nothing. Also, bearing in mind that philosophy will always have a multitude of contrary standpoints, *The Mountain Path* took substantially longer to write than my other books. I called upon the knowledge of a whole host of people, some living, but many long dead, by way of their books and texts.

I gained much useful knowledge for *The Mountain Path* from my lecturer in Asian Philosophy at the University of Tasmania, Dr Sonam Thakchoe, and the Central University of Tibetan Studies in Sarnath, Uttar Pradesh, which I attended in 2015.

My gratitude must go to the AMP Foundation for awarding me a grant from the Tomorrow Fund. Without their generosity it may well have been impossible for me to make a start. Thank you. I am also grateful to Arts Tasmania and the Regional Access Fund of Australia for their generosity. Plus, the support of Kaz Ross, Steph Calahan and Danielle Wood.

Likewise, I would like to thank the Banff Centre for Arts and Creativity for support of my project through its Mountain and Wilderness Writing programme. My personal faculty editor while there, Marni Jackson, did a fine job, and taught me how to use apostrophe's correctly. Many thanks also to the other MWW editors, Tony Whittome and Harley Rustad. Also, my fellow writers, Meghan Moya Finn, Fiona McGlynn, Chris Kassar, Emily Chappell, Eileen Keen, Jim Davidson, Ailsa Ross and Christina Reynolds. Your critiques were invaluable.

For the Totem Pole climb I would like to express my deep gratitude to Catherine Pettman and Matthew Newton of Rummin Productions for filming what would become *Doing It Scared*. It seems to have become a tradition with my books to thank Steve Monks ... so Steve Monks, what a star you are. Added to this, I would like to show my appreciation to Vonna Keller, Jeffrey Blake, Zoe Wilkinson, John Middendorf, David Ross, Andy Kuylaars, Andy Cianchi and Margie Jenkin for acting as mules and ensuring my safety out there. Plus, Peter Curtis and David Fraser for sound and additional camera, and Rian Taylor, Tom Waugh and Gene Millar at Ignite Digi for their superb aerial footage.

The directional support of ABC's Australian Story producer Rebecca Latham was invaluable in getting my conception compass aligned with the Totem Pole. And while we're on the subject of the Totem Pole I cannot go past Celia Bull and Neale Smith, without whom I wouldn't be around to ponder the meaning of life, death and the universe.

For Tibet, I would like to thank my cycling partner, the weapon that is Carol Hurst. And Sharyn Jones and Chris Jones for making *The Journey*, such a great little film. Plus Samdrup Tshering, Mel Weber and Jamphel Sonam for support. I wish to thank Paul Kronenberg and Sabriye Tenberken of Braille Without Borders and Kanthari too. I appreciate the help of Anita Pryor and Pete Rae at Adventure Works for opening my eyes to the amazing results Bush Adventure Therapy has on the disenfranchised in Australia.

For offering advice and thoughts on the text I am very much indebted to my readers. These were George Smith, Neville Rodman, David Roberts, John Middendorf, John and Geraldine Palmer, Tim McFadden and Dave Barnes. I am truly grateful. I must also express my gratitude to Ian Lonsdale and Cam Burns for advice. And I remain forever grateful to Ken Wilson and Harold Woolley, may they rest in peace, for believing in my writing, and getting me started on this Mountain Path. I also wish to thank my editor, Ed Douglas, for his encouragement and editorial advice.

Many thanks to Hazel Findlay for taking the time to write a thoughtful foreword.

My gratitude goes out to the photographers: Matthew Newton, Bill Hatcher, Melinda Oogjes, Paul Williams, Lynwen Griffiths and Dave Brown of Bamboo Chicken Productions, Sharyn Jones, Davide Negretti, Margie Jenkin, David Fraser, George Smith and the Royal Hobart Hospital.

Huge thanks also to Johnny Dawes, Lynn Hill, Geoff Powter and Greg Child for their words on the cover.

I offer my love and appreciation to my mother, Jean Allen, and the youngsters in my life, Cadi Pritchard, Eli Pritchard and Veve Fry. And I cherish the contribution of my partner, Melinda Oogjes. We had many intense philosophical discussions over the course of my writing of this book.

Finally, I acknowledge the gift of responsibility that the traditional custodians of the land have bestowed upon us, the land on which we all walk.

Paul Pritchard
www.paulpritchard.com.au

ABOUT THE AUTHOR

Paul Pritchard is an award-winning author and one of the UK's most visionary and accomplished climbers. Originally from Lancashire, he began climbing in his teens and went on to repeat some of the most difficult routes in the country, before moving to North Wales where he played a pivotal role in the development of the Dinorwig slate quarries and the imposing Gogarth cliffs on Anglesey. A move into mountaineering followed, with significant ascents around the world, including the East Face of the Central Tower of Paine in Patagonia, and the first ascent of the West Face of Mount Asgard on Baffin Island. In 1998 his life changed dramatically when he was hit by a falling rock while climbing the Totem Pole, a sea stack off the Tasmanian coast. He was left with hemiplegia – paralysis down the right side of his body – and also lost the power of speech for many months. Since his accident, Paul has continued to lead a challenging life through caving, tricycle racing, sea kayaking, river rafting, climbing Kilimanjaro, and, in 2009, a return to lead rock climbing. He is an international speaker, advocating for disability, and a diversity and inclusion trainer volunteering for The Human Library, which challenges the harmful effects of stereotyping and prejudice. He is the author of three books – *Deep Play, The Totem Pole*, and *The Longest Climb* – and has won the prestigious Boardman Tasker Prize on two occasions (*Deep Play*, 1997; *The Totem Pole*, 1999). *The Totem Pole* was also awarded the Grand Prize at the 1999 Banff Mountain Book Festival. Paul lives in Hobart, Tasmania.

CPSIA information can be obtained
at www.ICGtesting.com
Printed in the USA
JSHW021421070423
40074JS00002B/13